CHRISTINE DELPHY

Stevi Jackson

SAGE Publications
London • Thousand Oaks • New Delhi

First published 1996

SAGE Publications Ltd
6 Bonhill Street
London EC2A 4PU

SAGE Publications Inc
2455 Teller Road
Thousand Oaks, CA 91320

SAGE Publications India Pvt Ltd
32, M-Block Market
Greater Kailash – I
New Delhi 110 048

British Library Cataloguing in Publication data

A catalogue record for this book is available from the British Library.

ISBN 0 8039 8869 9
ISBN 0 8039 8870 2 (pbk)

Library of Congress catalog record available

Typeset by M Rules
Printed in Great Britain by Hartnolls Ltd, Bodmin, Cornwall

Contents

Preface

This series introduces readers to the life, times and work of key 'women of ideas' whose work has influenced people and helped change the times in which they lived. Some people might claim that there are few significant women thinkers. However, a litany of the women whose work is discussed in the first titles to be published gives the lie to this: Simone de Beauvoir, Zora Neale Hurston, Simone Weil, Olive Schreiner, Hannah Arendt, Eleanor Rathbone, Christine Delphy, Adrienne Rich, Audre Lorde, to be followed by Rosa Luxemburg, Melanie Klein, Mary Wollstonecraft, Andrea Dworkin and Catherine MacKinnon, Margaret Mead, Charlotte Perkins Gilman, Helene Cixous, Luce Irigaray and Julia Kristeva, Alexandra Kollontai, and others of a similar stature.

Every reader will want to add their own women of ideas to this list – which proves the point. There *are* major bodies of ideas and theories which women have originated; there *are* significant women thinkers; *but* women's intellectual work, like women's other work, is not taken so seriously nor evaluated so highly as men's. It may be men's perceptions of originality and importance which have shaped the definition and evaluation of women's work, but this does not constitute (nor is there any reason to regard it as) a definitive or universal standard. *Women of Ideas* exists to help change such perceptions, by taking women's past and present production of ideas seriously, and by introducing them to a wide new audience. *Women of Ideas* titles include women whose work is well-known from both the past and the present, and also those unfamiliar to modern readers although renowned among their contemporaries. The aim is to make their work accessible by drawing out of what is a frequently diverse and complex body of writing the central ideas and key themes, not least by locating these in relation to the intellectual, political and personal milieux in which this work originated.

Do women of ideas have 'another voice', one distinctive and different from that of men of ideas? or is this an essentialist claim and are ideas at basis unsexed? Certainly women's ideas are differently positioned with regard to their perception and evaluation. It is still a case of women having to be twice as good to be seen as half as good as men, for the apparatus of knowledge/power is configured in ways which do not readily accord women and their work the same status as that of men. However, this does not necessarily mean either that the ideas produced by women are significantly different in kind or, even if they presently are, that this is anything other than the product of the workings of social systems which systematically differentiate between the sexes, with such differences disappearing in an equal and just society. *Women of Ideas* is, among other things, a means of standing back and taking the longer view on such questions, with the series as a whole constituting one of the means of evaluating the 'difference debates', as its authors explore the contributions made by the particular women of ideas that individual titles focus upon.

Popularly, ideas are treated as the product of 'genius', of individual minds inventing what is startlingly original – and absolutely unique to them. However, within feminist thought a different approach is taken, seeing ideas as social products rather than uniquely individual ones, as collective thoughts albeit uttered in the distinctive voices of particular individuals. Here there is a recognition that ideas have a 'historical moment' when they assume their greatest significance – and that 'significance' is neither transhistorical nor transnational, but is rather temporally and culturally specific, so that the 'great ideas' of one time and place can seem commonplace or ridiculous in others. Here too the cyclical and social nature of the life of ideas is recognised, in which 'new' ideas may in fact be 'old' ones in up-to-date language and expression.

And, perhaps most importantly for the *Women of Ideas* series, there is also a recognition of the frequently *gendered* basis of the judgements of the 'significance' and 'importance' of ideas and bodies of work.

The title of the series is taken from Dale Spender's (1982) *Women of Ideas, and What Men have Done to Them*. 'What men have done to them' is shorthand for a complex process in which bodies of ideas 'vanish', not so much by being deliberately suppressed (although this has happened) as by being trivialised, misrepresented, excluded from the canon of what is deemed good, significant, great. In addition to these gatekeeping processes, there are other broader factors at work. Times change, intellectual fashion changes also. One product of this is the often very different interpretation and understanding of bodies of ideas over time: when looked at from different – unsympathetic – viewpoints, then dramatic shifts in the representation of these can occur. Such shifts in intellectual fashion sometimes occur in their own right, while at other times they are related to wider social, economic and political changes in the world. Wars, the expansion and then contraction of colonialism, revolutions, all have had an effect on what people think, how ideas are interpreted and related to, which ideas are seen as important and which outmoded.

'Women of ideas' of course need not necessarily position themselves as feminists nor prioritise concern with gender. The terms 'feminist' and 'woman' are by no means to be collapsed, but they are not to be treated as binaries either. Some major female thinkers focus on the human condition in order to rethink the nature of reality and thus of 'knowledge'. In doing so they also re-position the nature of ideas. Each of the women featured has produced ideas towards that greater whole which is a more comprehensive 'rethinking of the nature of knowledge. These women have produced ideas which form bodies of systematic thought, as they have pursued trains of thought over the course of their individual lives. This is not to suggest that such ideas give expression to a 'universal essence' in the way Plato proposed. It is instead to reject rigidly dividing 'realist' from 'idealist' from 'materialist', recognising that aspects of these supposedly categorical distinctions can be brought together to illuminate the extraordinarily complex and fascinating process by which ideas are produced and reproduced in particular intellectual, cultural and historical contexts.

The *Women of Ideas* series is, then, concerned with the 'history of ideas'. It recognises the importance of the 'particular voice' as well as the shared context; it insists on the relevance of the thinker as well as that which is thought. It is concerned with individuals in their relation to wider collectivities and contexts, and it focuses upon the role of particular women of ideas without 'personifying' or individualising the processes by which ideas are shaped, produced, changed. It emphasises that there is a history of '*mentalités collectives*', recognising the continuum between the everyday and the elite, between 'commonsense' and 'high theory'. Ideas have most meaning in their use, in the way they influence other minds and wider social processes, something which occurs by challenging and changing patterns of understanding. As well as looking at the impact of particular women of ideas, the series brings their work to a wider audience, to encourage a greater understanding of the contribution of these women to the way that we *do* think – and also the way that we perhaps *should* think – about knowledge and the human condition.

Liz Stanley

Acknowledgements

I would like to thank all of those who have contributed to bringing this project to fruition. Diana Leonard has offered advice from the outset and provided me with invaluable background information. She also made her translations of Delphy's recent work available to me prior to publication. I received additional help with translation from Claire Hadfield. Liz Stanley provided constructive comments on the draft of the manuscript; both she and Karen Phillips at Sage have been consistently supportive, especially during the more difficult phases of writing. Friends and colleagues, at the University of Strathclyde and elsewhere, have encouraged me in numerous ways. I owe particular personal debts to Pauline Young, Sue Scott and Shaun Moores. Finally, I could not have written this book without the cooperation of Christine Delphy herself, her willingness to discuss her work with me and her patience with my endless queries. Needless to say, the interpretations of events and ideas are my own, and I bear the responsibility for any errors, omissions and biases this entails.

Stevi Jackson

1

Christine Delphy: Activist and Theorist

Christine Delphy is a French radical feminist theorist and activist whose writings span the period from the earliest days of second wave feminism to the present. Her work has always been controversial and she continues to make challenging contributions to current feminist debates. She began to develop her distinctive perspective – materialist feminism – in the context of the French movement in the late 1960s and early 1970s, and has always retained the political commitment which provided her inspiration. While her ideas grew from her experience of feminist politics, they also bear the marks of her academic background. Her training as a sociologist predisposed her to seek explanations for women's subordination in terms of social structure – the institutionalized relationships and hierarchies characteristic of a particular society which shape the lives of its members. She found a framework for her analysis in marxism, which might seem rather unusual for a radical feminist, but her application of marxism is far from conventional. In focusing on patriarchy, the structures through which men dominate and exploit women, she departs radically from the more usual marxist emphasis on capitalism and the exploitation of the working class. Her materialism also sets her apart from another form of theory which has emerged from France – psychoanalytic explorations of feminine language and subjectivity. This latter tendency dominates the image of French feminism in the English-speaking world, belying the diversity of feminist thought which actually exists in France (Duchen, 1986, 1987).

In this first chapter I will provide some details of Delphy's life as a theorist and activist, placing the development of her ideas in the context of the French feminist movement. In so doing I want to make it clear that she is not an isolated exponent of her views, but is part of a wider current of French radical feminist theorists. I will also explore the connections between her theory and her politics – connections which Delphy herself thinks vitally important. She has always maintained that feminist knowledge should serve the political interests of the women's movement. The question of how those interests should be defined, however, has been much debated within modern feminism and emerged as a central issue from the earliest days of the movement in France.

The making of a feminist

Christine Delphy was born in Paris in 1941. She studied sociology at the Sorbonne, where she gained a Licenciée de Sociologie in 1961 and the Etudes des Supérieures in 1962. She then went to the USA to continue her graduate studies, first at the University of Chicago and subsequently at the University of California at Berkeley. In 1964 she left university to do civil rights work, having gained a fellowship from the Eleanor Roosevelt Foundation for Human Relations for that purpose. It was through her involvement in the civil rights movement that she began to envisage the possibility of a feminist movement. Like many women who were politically active in the 1960s, she became aware that the oppression of women was absent from the agenda of liberation movements and hence of the need for women to organize themselves. Yet at that time, before the resurgence of feminism, the idea that women could create their own autonomous movement was revolutionary. Delphy says that she was convinced that others would think her 'crazy' for entertaining such a notion.[1] One person to whom she confided her vision was Emmanuèle de Lesseps, whom she met in the USA. Back in France, the two became firm friends and long-term political allies.

Following her return to Paris in 1966, Delphy took up a post as a research assistant at the Centre Nationale de Reserche Scientifique (CNRS). Here, in 1968, she met Jacqueline Feldman-Hogasen who told her of a small group called 'Féminin-Masculin-Avenir' (FMA), which Delphy and Lesseps joined. The FMA had been founded in the autumn of 1967 by Feldman-Hogasen and Anne Zelensky (also known as Anne Tristan) and was later to become one of the key groups from which the embryonic French women's movement developed (Delphy, 1991b; Tristan and Pisan, 1977). The summer of 1968 was a high point of radical activism in the Western world, particularly in Paris. In May and June 1968, mass students' and workers' strikes brought normal French life to a standstill and huge demonstrations took over the streets of Paris. To the young radicals of that generation, it seemed for a brief euphoric moment as if capitalism were about to fall. Women's liberation, however, was still not an issue for most of the left. Members of the FMA sought to raise 'the question of women', organizing numerous debates through which they increased their membership. At its height, in June 1968, it still had only 40 or so members, about half of whom were men and, once the revolutionary fervour of 1968 died down, their numbers dwindled (Delphy, 1991b).

For the next two years they organized weekly discussion meetings during which time Delphy began to develop her materialist position. Her research at the CNRS, on patterns of inheritance in peasant families, was alerting her to the economic inequalities within families and also to the ways in which traditional economics concerned itself only with the market. She was also determined to find an explanation for women's subordination which did not rely on assumptions about 'natural' distinctions between the sexes. On the left, of course, Marx's work was much discussed, but usually only in relation to class politics. Delphy recalls her annoyance at a remark by one of the men in the FMA which seems to have acted as a catalyst in her thinking:

> He claimed that the oppression of women could not be equal in importance to that of the male proletariat since, he said, although women

> were oppressed, they were not 'exploited'. I was well aware that there was something wrong with this formulation. In that group at least we recognized that women earn half as much as men and work twice as hard: but apparently their oppression had, in theory, no economic dimension! (Delphy, 1984: 15)

By the time the FMA made contact with other women's groups in 1970, Delphy was arguing that women constituted an exploited class and that male civilization was sustained by women's unacknowledged, unpaid labour (Tristan and Pisan, 1987: 37). This was to become the central tenet of the theories she subsequently elaborated. She had also persuaded the group that women's liberation was an issue in its own right, not merely secondary to class politics. This position had been incorporated into a manifesto written collectively by the FMA: 'We refuse to allow the search for a solution to the female "problem" to be subordinated to the workers' or students' movements' (quoted in Tristan and Pisan, 1987: 36). She had been less successful in convincing the others of the logical corollary of this – that women should organize autonomously in women only groups: 'We could not bring ourselves to agree with her, clinging falsely to our idealistic notions. Liberation was an issue which concerned men and women: why be divided in what was a battle to be united?' (Tristan and Pisan, 1987: 36). In fact most of the men left the FMA anyway and by 1970 only two remained (Tristan and Pisan, 1977, 1987), along with four women members – Anne Zelensky, Jacqueline Feldman-Hogasen, Emmanuèle de Lesseps and Christine Delphy (Delphy, 1991b). The meaning of the initials FMA had meanwhile changed to 'Féminisme-Marxisme-Action', reflecting their increased radicalism.

Over the period 1968–70 other small groups were meeting in France, each unaware of the others' existence. By 1969 news of the American women's liberation movement began to reach them, making them more optimistic, but the potential for such a movement in France was yet to be realized: 'In the French political climate of that time, such an idea was anathema to all men and even to most women. For the vast majority of self-defined progressives the idea of a feminist organization, especially one that excluded men, was simply unthinkable' (Beauvoir, 1985: 233). But when two other women's groups finally met with the FMA in 1970, they helped create the impetus for a wider feminist movement. One of these, the *Oreilles Vertes* ('green ears'), is often mentioned in histories of this period, but little seems to be known about them. Anne Tristan describes them as academic women, all married, who had formed a consciousness raising group on the basis of their shared experience of the unfair division of domestic labour (Tristan and Pisan, 1987). The other group, consisting of eight women who had been meeting since September 1969,[2] was far more politically significant in terms of the tendencies which were to develop within the French movement. It included among its members Monique Wittig, who was to become a prominent radical feminist, and Antionette Fouque, who founded the group known as *Psychanalyse et Politique* or *Psych et Po* (Delphy, 1991b).

The birth of the MLF

The MLF came into being in 1970. At the beginning of the year there were a few small women's groups, unconnected to each other. By the autumn, hundreds were meeting regularly at the *Beaux Arts* (the school of fine art) in Paris. Certain key events marked the emergence of the movement: the publication of an article entitled 'Combat pour la liberation de la femme'[3] in *L'idiot international*, a left-wing monthly paper, a demonstration at Vincennes, another at L'Arc de Triomphe and the publication of a special feminist issue of the journal *Partisans* (Delphy, 1991b; Duchen, 1986; Tristan and Pisan, 1977). Delphy and her friends found themselves witnessing and participating in the launching of a new movement.

The article in *L'idiot*, exposing what it called women's 'servitude' and calling for a women's liberation movement, was published in May 1970. It was signed, using first names only, by Gille and Monique Wittig, Marcia Rothenberg and Margaret Stephenson (Delphy, 1991b). There was, according to Anne Tristan (Zelensky), 'great excitement in the FMA' at the appearance of an article 'we could so easily have written ourselves' (Tristan and Pisan, 1987: 33). They wrote to the authors, care of *L'idiot*, but received no reply. They subsequently discovered why. The article had been written by four members of a group who were split politically over whether priority should be given to women's struggle or the class struggle. The lines of cleavage which were to divide the movement were already present in this group, the article's authors taking the former position, Antionette Fouque and her supporters adopting the latter stance and dissociating themselves from the article. Fouque, in particular, argued against any attempt to enlarge their numbers or make public statements until they had fully developed their own analysis of women's oppression. Monique Wittig later told Delphy that Fouque had advised against replying to the FMA on the grounds that the latter was a reformist group (Delphy, 1991b).

At around the same time, students at the University of Paris at Vincennes organized a demonstration and meeting for which they had made banners and T-shirts bearing the words 'Libération des femmes, Année Zéro' and the feminist logo already adopted in the USA – a women's symbol with a clenched fist at its centre. Wittig and her group were involved in this event (Delphy, 1991b). Meanwhile, a letter from the FMA had been published in *Le Nouvel Observateur*. Among the replies they received was one from the *Oreilles Vertes* requesting a meeting, which was duly arranged. Prior to this meeting, Delphy recalls, she received a phone call from one Antionette Fouque, who was at that time unknown to her. Fouque introduced herself by saying that she belonged to the group who had written the article in *L'idiot* and organized the demonstration at Vincennes but then went on to say that she was not one of those who had written the article and organized the demonstration! Delphy soon realized that this woman held a 'class struggle' perspective, but nonetheless told her of the meeting with the *Oreilles Vertes* (Delphy, 1991b: 141).

Fouque appeared at the meeting along with Jo Chanel, but Delphy and Tristan recall that only Fouque spoke (Delphy, 1991b; Tristan and Pisan, 1987). A further meeting was arranged between the three groups, and it was finally agreed that all future meetings would exclude men. This next meeting proved critical, for it was the point at which the existing small groups ceased to meet separately, becoming merged into a new, larger, group. It also became clear at this meeting that there were irreconcilable differences within the embryonic movement. There were over 30 women present, the largest gathering of feminists that most of them had experienced, at least within France. The discussion centred on a manifesto prepared by the women from the FMA, which Anne Zelensky read out. The first point of controversy was the term feminist, which the women from the FMA used to describe themselves. 'We saw ourselves as the direct spiritual descendants of the suffragettes, especially as far as the use of direct action was concerned' (Tristan and Pisan, 1987: 35), although opportunities for such action had not yet materialized. Fouque, however, damned the suffragettes as 'bourgeois' women who were interested only in gaining privileges for women of their own class, and who had no sense of solidarity with working class women. For Fouque, feminism was not revolutionary because it was not defined in terms of class solidarity (Tristan and Pisan, 1987: 35–6). Fouque also contested the central tenet of the manifesto, a point which Delphy had personally developed: that women's struggle should not be subordinated to class struggle (Tristan and Pisan, 1977, 1987).

Tristan gives a detailed account of this meeting, and of the heated debate which ensued between Delphy and Fouque (Tristan and Pisan, 1987: 34–7). Delphy countered the claim that solidarity with the working class was a primary objective by arguing that solidarity should not mean subordinating feminist aims to the class struggle, that all forms of oppression should be given equal weight and that the liberation of women required the overthrow of patriarchy, not simply capitalism. Fouque asked: 'you're surely not going to try and suggest that women form a homogeneous class?', to which Delphy replied: 'Yes, I'm saying exactly that', going on to explain that women formed a category of oppressed individuals, with common characteristics and shared political interests in relation to men as a social group (Tristan and Pisan, 1987: 37). Tristan tells us that the discussion polarized opinion into those for and against the position Delphy was arguing, with the majority following Fouque. Delphy had, however, one influential and vocal supporter from within Fouque's group – Monique Wittig.[4] The alliance that began that evening was to last almost a decade. More generally the meeting gave rise to the groupings which were to dominate the MLF in the coming years.

Toril Moi comments that the fact that a meeting of 'would-be feminist activists . . . only managed to launch an acrimonious theoretical debate, would seem to mark the situation as typically "French" in its apparent insistence on the primacy of theory over politics' (1987: 3). This statement, however, overstates the particularity of French feminism. It is true to say that similar divisions arose wherever women came to feminist politics from a prior involvement in the left. The same tendencies, for example, emerged in Britain, but without the association – which was to become apparent in France – between a version of the class-struggle position and psychoanalytic theory. Moreover, more was at stake than theory, for the disagreements also concerned priorities for political action. Nonetheless, although the meeting was far from harmonious, it marked the beginning of the new feminist movement in France. As Tristan puts it: 'something important had happened that night. Something was in the process of being born anew. And whether my companions liked it or not, that something was definitely feminism' (Tristan and Pisan, 1987: 37).

At this stage according to Delphy, the women from the FMA, the signatories of the article in *L'idiot* and many others 'had only one idea in our heads: to contact other women, to set up a movement' (1991b: 142). They were opposed in this by Fouque and her allies, who argued that meetings should remain closed until they had developed a deeper analysis and that any public events would be premature (1991b). Delphy and her friends, however, were determined to make feminism into a political force. A small group of them, by virtue of one spectacular action, succeeded in giving the movement a public identity. They had heard of a women's strike to be organized by American feminists on 26 August and decided to make a gesture of solidarity. August is not an auspicious month for organizing political action in France. It is the national holiday period in which Paris almost shuts down and many of its inhabitants leave for the countryside. A number of the newly-formed feminist group were students who had returned home for the vacation, others were foreigners who feared deportation if they were arrested (Delphy, 1991b). They could therefore muster only a handful of women, so their action had to be symbolic and guaranteed to attract maximum publicity. Anne Tristan, who had just returned from Cuba and was therefore not party to the clandestine arrangements, recalls being wakened on the morning of the 26 August by a telephone call from 'Mano' (Emmanuèle de Lesseps), who told her they were taking action in support of the American feminists and to meet them at a café in the Champs Elysees at noon:

> Christine and Monique were there. They had brought a gigantic wreath which they intended to place on the tomb of the unknown soldier with ribbons bearing the words: 'One man in two is a woman', 'There is always someone even more unknown than the soldier: his wife.' (Tristan and Pisan, 1987: 39)

They never reached the tomb at L'Arc de Triomphe. As soon as they set out, the police arrested them and confiscated the wreath. They were released two hours later. They did, however, receive the publicity they hoped for. They had invited journalists and they had chosen their target well. As Marks and Courtivron put it:

> The tomb of the unknown soldier occupies a sacred place within the French symbolic order and within Western mythology. Located in the centre of Paris it signifies patriotism, nationalism and the masculine virtues of heroism and courage. The Arc de Triomphe is one of the most explicit signs of a French, and, by extension, a victorious, universal male order. (1981: 31)

The wreath challenged all this, and the press reacted 'as if a sacrilege had been committed'(1981: 31). Many papers exaggerated the scale of the demonstration – one even claiming that a thousand women had been present, but in fact there were only nine of them: Cathy Bernheim, Monique Bourroux, Frédérique Daber, Christine Delphy, Emmanuèle de Lesseps, Christiane Rochefort, Janine Sert, Monique Wittig and Anne Zelensky, but they had achieved what they wanted. The next day *Le Figaro* and *L'Aurore* announced the birth of the 'Mouvement de libération de la femme française' (Delphy, 1991b: 143). They were referred to as a movement to liberate woman (la femme) rather than women (des femmes), but that mattered less than the fact that they now had a public existence, that 'for the first time the women's liberation movement was a talking point' (Tristan and Pisan, 1987: 39).

This was not the only activity these women were involved with over the summer. They were engaged in preparing a special issue of the journal *Partisans* entitled *Libération des femmes année O*. Originally it had been planned around the contributions of a number of male experts, and it had taken protracted negotiations to convince the editor that an issue of the journal devoted to women should be written by women. In the end, the feminists themselves were given considerable control over it and it finally appeared in print in October 1970. It was a landmark publication, 'the first feminist review to appear after years, decades even, of silence' (Tristan and Pisan, 1987: 38). This initiative was also opposed by Fouque and her associates and they declined to contribute anything to it (Delphy, 1991b). Among other contributions, it included Delphy's essay 'The Main Enemy', now recognized as a feminist classic and still her single best known work. Here Delphy developed the arguments she had incorporated into the FMA manifesto: that women shared a common oppression, that men exploited women's labour within families and benefited directly from this exploitation and that women constituted a class (see Chapters 3 and 4).

In September the first general assembly of the new movement was held. Over a hundred women came and with each subsequent meeting the numbers grew. The meetings were chaotic. Feminists in France, as elsewhere, rejected the structured procedures and hierarchical organization typical of both conventional politics and the male-dominated far left. The divisions continued, centred still on the priority which should be given to feminism vis-à-vis the class struggle. Some condemned the demonstration at L'Arc de Triomphe as 'apolitical' and 'petty bourgeois' (Tristan and Pisan, 1977, 1987). From Tristan's account, it appears that those arguing for the 'class struggle' position now included not only Fouque's supporters, but also women from more conventional left groups. Those committed to feminist action found these meetings frustrating: the same discussions were being continually rehearsed and little progress was being made (Delphy, 1991b; Tristan and Pisan, 1977). A breakaway radical feminist group was formed in October 1970, originally called *Les Petites Marguerites* and later *Féministes Révolutionnaires*,[5] in which both Delphy and Wittig were prominent activists. Although they only met separately for a few months – by which time opposing tendencies had also abandoned the general assemblies – they remained an influential grouping within the MLF for the next few years and were responsible for some of its more spectacular and successful actions.

French radical feminism in the 1970s

The first few years of the 1970s were crucial ones for the MLF. It was a time when the movement grew rapidly, new issues were constantly being identified, major campaigns were launched and the main theoretical and political tendencies within the movement became defined. This was when feminist activism was most visible and public: after this time the movement fragmented and became less easily identifiable as a single movement. Delphy remembers these early years as a period during which the movement was her life. She was involved in most of the major feminist events in Paris, was at meetings almost every night and spent most of her free time with other feminists, exchanging ideas and planning future actions. It was in this context, and in conjunction with other radical feminists, that she developed further her distinctive theoretical position. By the end of the decade she had published a number of articles defining her materialist feminism in relation to other perspectives and continued to write extensively on women's exploitation within families. Her writing abilities were also put to use within the movement, drafting innumerable leaflets and statements, and occasional anonymous articles, on behalf of the campaigns she was involved in.

Radical feminism emerged as one of three main currents within the MLF in the 1970s, the other two being socialist feminists and *Psych et Po* (see Beauvoir, 1985; Duchen, 1986). Not all women, however, saw themselves as attached to any particular tendency and many who identified themselves as feminists would work with different groups on different projects (Picq, 1987). The opposition between radical feminists and socialist feminists was similar to that evident in most other Western nations at the time, with the former prioritizing women's struggle against patriarchy, while the latter emphasized solidarity with the working class in the struggle against capitalism and from 1971 organized separately from the wider women's movement under the banner *Libération des femmes, tendence lutte de classes* ('women's liberation, class struggle tendency'). Many of these women belonged to various marxist and Trotskyist groups. There were differences among them in the degree of credence they gave to feminism and the extent to which they were willing to subordinate feminism to class issues. Some certainly felt a conflict of interests between their feminism and their socialism (Duchen, 1986). Socialist feminists campaigned around such issues as equal pay and women's right to work, but joined with radical feminists around some issues, such as abortion (Beauvoir, 1985).

Psych et Po, the group founded and led by Antionette Fouque, is a peculiarly French phenomenon. For all Fouque's rhetoric about class struggle in early MLF meetings, the approach she fostered had little to do with struggle – in the sense of political action – at all. Rather, the group engaged in introspective investigations into female subjectivity, as Fouque herself put it, an 'underground, anonymous practice: moles' (1987: 51). Their main theoretical perspective was not marxism but psychoanalysis, through which they sought to recover femininity from its repression within a patriarchal, phallocentric symbolic order. Their goal was 'to bring women into existence', to nurture their radical 'alterity' or 'otherness', to win women's independence from the masculine symbolic order which currently traps us. *Psych et Po* consistently declared itself opposed to feminism, which it saw simply as women seeking to take men's places in a 'phallocratic society' without changing it (Fouque, 1987: 52). They even descended on an international women's day demonstration bearing placards carrying the message 'down with feminism' (Duchen, 1986). Despite their stated preference for an anonymous mole-like existence, *Psych et Po* became a successful commercial enterprise. In 1973 they set up a publishing company and in 1974 opened the first of a chain of book shops, both called *des femmes* ('women'). In 1979 they registered the name Mouvement de libération des femmes as their company property and the logo MLF as their trademark. They thus declared themselves the official women's liberation movement and prevented other women using its name and initials – and successfully defended this move against legal action taken by other women (Beauvoir, 1985; Duchen, 1986, 1987; Kaplan, 1992;

Marks and Courtivron, 1981). If this achieved nothing else, it united all other currents within the women's movement against them.

Needless to say, radical feminists were consistently critical of *Psych et Po*'s theory and practice throughout the 1970s. It was largely in opposition to them that French radical feminists developed their own theoretical and political position. This is one reason why they were less willing than some feminists elsewhere to consider women's biological characteristics as contributing to their oppression:

> In France those analyses which accord a biology a significant role in shaping women's oppression are linked to such politically reactionary positions as those of the group Psych et Po., which believes that women, rather than being 'oppressed,' are '*re*pressed,' that the female self has been denied expression by men and that liberation should be sought in the reaffirmation of women's uniquely 'female nature.' (Beauvoir, 1985: 235–6)

In contrast, radical feminists insisted that there was no female (or male) 'nature', that masculinity and femininity were the product of a patriarchal society. Their understanding of gender differences as socially constructed was associated with the position that men and women were defined by their class relationship to each other. Seeing men and women as classes also distinguished them from socialist feminists who thought of class only in terms of proletarians and capitalists. However, radical and socialist feminists shared a commitment to political activism, and this distanced both from *Psych et Po*, whose main aim was to work on themselves and develop their perspective through self-analysis. In contrast, radical feminists 'wanted to burst into the world with as much noise and attention as possible' (Duchen, 1986: 16). The aim of the latter was to bring women's oppression into the public arena in order to mobilize a feminist movement.

Unlike *Psych et Po*, radical feminists were not a coherent organized body, but rather a loose network of groups, campaigns and individuals. Even named groupings, like the *Féministes Révolutionnaires*, had no formal structure or leadership. They remained committed to principles which they saw as fundamental to the feminist movement – that it should be an autonomous movement, that it should have no rules or hierarchies and that it should be an extra-parliamentary movement using direct action as its main political weapon. The radical feminist emphasis on the autonomy of the movement and their insistence that women were a class is sometimes even now misunderstood. Gisela Kaplan (1992), for example sees the radical feminists as being lesbian separatists from the start. Although they included among their ranks some avowed lesbians, such as Christine Delphy and Monique Wittig, there were many others who had not publicly proclaimed their lesbianism or who were, like Anne Zelensky and Emmanuèle de Lesseps, openly heterosexual. Certainly they raised issues of sexuality, exposed heterosexual privilege and opposed the oppression of lesbians, but radical lesbianism – the idea that feminists should eschew all relationships with men – did not become an issue until the end of the decade, when it provoked a fundamental split within French radical feminism (Duchen, 1987).

In the early 1970s the radical feminists continued their practice of organizing spectacular events to publicize their aims, but they also began to organize major campaigns around abortion and violence against women – initiatives in which Delphy was an active participant. In November 1970 they infiltrated and disrupted the 'National Assembly of Women' hosted by the magazine *Elle*. This provided them with the opportunity to gain publicity for the MLF and put forward a feminist perspective within an event designed as a celebration of traditional femininity. At the opening reception of the 'assembly', they took over the platform and made a statement of their own, opposed to the aims of the conference. They also read out a lampoon of a questionnaire previously circulated by *Elle*. A question on whether women were more or less able than men to drive a car was replaced by: 'In your opinion do double X chromosomes contain the genes of double declutching?' (Duchen, 1986: 10). Other questions were added such as:

> When you are pregnant and don't want to keep the child, which option do you choose:
>
> – knitting needles,
> – a vine branch,
> – iron, copper or bronze barbed wire,
> – street walking to raise 2000F? (Tristan and Pisan, 1987: 43)

This earned them some rather distorted press coverage – *Le Figaro* described them as 'awesome amazons with close-cropped hair', when all had long hair (Tristan and Pisan, 1987: 43). Their activities at the assembly, however, had a more serious side. They set up a stall selling their issue of *Partisans* and took part in a discussion of abortion on demand.

After this event some of the women began to feel that they wanted to do something of more lasting consequence, and the issue they chose was abortion. Although committed to direct, extra-parliamentary action, radical feminists did not back away from pressing for reform where this was of immediate benefit to women. The successful campaign to legalize abortion was a case in point. Both contraception and abortion were illegal in France and for some feminists, in France as elsewhere, this lack of control over their own bodies was fundamental to women's oppression. In France, however, this was not initially a popular issue within the MLF. When Anne Zelensky and Christine Delphy first announced their intention to form an abortion group at a general meeting the response varied from lukewarm to hostile. Only four women, including Zelensky and Delphy, came to the first meeting of the abortion group, but word spread to women who did not attend the big general meetings and they were soon joined by a dozen or so more. Some of these were from left groups, others were unaligned women new to the movement (Tristan and Pisan, 1977, 1987). Delphy and Zelensky had already met journalists from the weekly magazine *Le Nouvel Observateur*, who suggested the idea of a women's manifesto on abortion signed by 'big names' (Tristan and Pisan, 1987: 46). When the idea was put to the group there were some predictable negative responses, women opposed to the use of 'celebrities' and 'collaboration with the bourgeois press' (Tristan and Pisan, 1987: 47), but most of the regular group members decided to go ahead with the idea. They began work on what became known as 'the manifesto of the 343' (343 women signed it), whose publication has since been recognized as a significant historical event for the MLF (Duchen, 1986; Kaplan, 1992; Marks and Courtivron, 1981).

Anne Zelensky contacted Simone de Beauvoir for help. Beauvoir, author of *The Second Sex* (1949), one of the few critiques of women's oppression to be published in the long years between the first and second waves of feminism, was an inspiration to many feminists in the 1970s, both within France and elsewhere. In France she was well respected as a novelist, philosopher and campaigner for left-wing causes.[6] Beauvoir agreed to head the signatories to the manifesto and to use her contacts to get other influential women to sign. She, Delphy and Rochefort were delegated the task of collecting signatures. What women were being asked to sign was no mere statement of support for abortion rights, but a declaration that they had broken the law. The text of the manifesto ran as follows:

> One million women have abortions in France each year. They do so in dangerous conditions because they are condemned to secrecy, although, if done under medical supervision, this operation is extremely simple. These millions of women are never mentioned. I declare that I am one of them. I declare that I have had an abortion. Just as we demand free access to contraception, we demand freedom to have abortions.[7]

The statement, with its 343 signatures, appeared in *Le Nouvel Observateur* on 5 April 1971 and was also published on the same day in *Le Monde*. Both papers published all the signatures, the unknown activists along with the well-known writers, film stars and public figures. In addition, *Le Nouvel Observateur* gave the feminist campaigners a page on which to express their own views about abortion and motherhood. Until the manifesto's publication, most of the women who attended the general assemblies of the MLF had been either sceptical about it or opposed to it. Now, however, it was enthusiastically supported. It had certainly succeeded in making abortion a public issue – the French press was full of discussion of the women who had admitted to having abortions, and foreign newspapers also covered the story. Hundreds of letters were flooding in from women wanting to add their signatures. There was an obvious need for a mass campaign.

Two organizations emerged which continued to press for freedom of abortion and contraception. Women among the 343, including Beauvoir, Rochefort and the lawyer Gisèle Halami, who had acted as a legal adviser as well as a signatory, formed the association known as *Choisir*. There was an immediate need to defend the 343 against possible prosecution (which in the event never happened) and to make use of the impetus provided by the manifesto. Although it had grown out of the feminist campaign, differences were soon to emerge between Halami, who became its effective leader, and feminists from the MLF. The Mouvement pour la Libération de l'Avortement (MLA) was a mixed campaign founded by the original abortion group which added contraception to its remit, making the acronym MLAC. Others joined the movement – for example there was a manifesto published by radical doctors in 1972. Partial victory came when abortion in the first ten weeks of pregnancy was legalized in 1975, for a trial period of five years. In 1979 the new law was given permanent status. This was not the total freedom to abortion that feminists had hoped for, but it was significant progress. In 1979, when the law was reviewed, thousands of women took to the streets demonstrating their support for it.

Delphy (1980a) has since commented on the necessity of recognizing that this victory was set in motion by the feminist movement. Despite the stir that the manifesto of the 343 caused at the time, the liberalization of abortion law has since been represented as something that simply happened as a result of the march of progress or as a result of parliamentary politics or as the individual act of the minister who drafted the new law, Simone Veil. Even within the women's movement this history can too easily be forgotten. Delphy recalls seeing a chronology of the campaign for abortion reform in a local women's group in 1976, in which it was said 'that the struggle began in 1972 . . . with the manifesto of the doctors'. Where, she asks, was the women-only, women's movement campaign? 'It was not there, only five years afterwards; it had been wiped out of its own history by a feminist group' (1987: 38). The lessons of this are important for Delphy, because the rewriting of history which had occurred here might serve to invalidate the basis of feminist politics – the importance of women organizing autonomously against their common oppression.

Abortion was never an isolated issue for feminists, but was part of a wider struggle against patriarchal domination. After the publication of the manifesto of the 343, those who had begun that initiative continued to be active around abortion, but soon began to broaden their focus. The 'days of denunciation of crimes against women', which took place the following year, grew out of the abortion campaign, but extended its scope to take in all forms of violence against women. The idea for a large rally, centred on women's personal testimonies, was first floated at an early meeting of *Choisir*. Differences soon emerged about how the rally should be organized and what form it should take. Halami favoured a staged performance taking the form of a trial with 'expert' witnesses. The women from the original abortion campaign wanted a more open feminist event, evoking on a larger scale the form of public declaration that the manifestation of the 343 had achieved. What in effect was happening was a clash between traditional modes of political organization and the relatively less structured practices of the MLF. Eventually Halami disassociated herself from it and planning went ahead along the lines the feminists had envisaged (Tristan and Pisan, 1977). There were disagreements among the feminists themselves. Delphy remembers arguing that the testimonies should be organized thematically, to illustrate particular political points, but was eventually won over to the more spontaneous form of organization, with each group preparing its own testimonies. The resulting two 'days of denunciation' on 13 and 14 May 1972 were a resounding success. Over 5,000 women were brought together at the Mutualité, one of the largest public venues in Paris. In addition to the sense of solidarity created by the sharing of women's experiences, the testimonies provided impetus for future campaigns and discussions, bringing into the political arena not only abortion – the issue which first inspired the event – but also motherhood, violence, rape and sexuality (Duchen, 1986; Tristan and Pisan, 1977).

Simone de Beauvoir remained involved in the 'days of denunciation' from its initial planning through to the event itself, marking an increased involvement with the new feminist movement which had begun with the manifesto of the 343. Delphy got to know Beauvoir during this period and developed a great deal of personal respect for her. What impressed her most was that Beauvoir never expected to be treated as a star or a leader. She came to feminist events not as a keynote speaker but as a participant; she came to listen and to learn rather than to impose her own views.

Nonetheless her influence and support proved useful to Delphy. Delphy's 'Protofeminism and anti-feminism' was published as the lead article in an edition of *Les Temps Moderns*, which Beauvoir edited, and the latter acted as titular editor of *Questions Féministes*, the radical feminist journal which Delphy helped found. Later, when the *Questions Féministes* collective split (see below) Beauvoir supported Delphy and Lesseps rather than the radical lesbians.

The year 1972 was a high point in feminist activism and visibility, certainly in Paris (Tristan and Pisan, 1977). In addition to the 'days of denunciation', feminists moblized around the trial of four women from the Paris suburb of Bobigny accused of procuring an abortion for the 11 year old daughter of one of them. Other events in that year included a demonstration against mothers' day in the Champs Elysées. The large open meetings in Paris continued to provide a forum for debate and a sense of belonging to a large movement. After 1972, however, these meetings were gradually abandoned, as *Psych et Po* once more began to exercise a disruptive influence (Beauvoir, 1985). The lack of a collective movement identity was exacerbated when *Le Torchon Brule*, a feminist magazine open to the whole movement, ceased publication after 1973. The movement subsequently became more diverse and fragmented. Different groups of women worked on different projects – running discussion groups, magazines, women's centres, refuges and rape crisis centres.

This fragmentation proved particularly problematic for radical feminists. Whereas *Psych et Po* was a tightly knit organization, and began to run magazines, bookshops and a publishing company, and socialist feminists organized through locally based groups, radical feminists had tended to group themselves around particular projects or discussion groups. This made them less visible and harder to locate by newcomers to the movement. The problem was solved in part by setting up women's centres, but these were often short lived (Beauvoir, 1985). Nonetheless radical feminists in general, and *Féministes Révolutionnaires* in particular, continued to be active around issues of sexuality and violence against women and continued to intervene in feminist events, putting their own position against both *Psych et Po* and socialist feminists. In 1976 they circulated a leaflet, drafted by Delphy, at the launching of a public anti-rape campaign (reprinted in rhodes and McNeil, 1985). Here they opposed sections of the left press who saw demands for the prosecution of rapists as 'reactionary' and as strengthening 'bourgeois justice'. They argued that, on the contrary, demanding that rape be taken seriously as a crime was part of an ideological struggle which revealed the patriarchal interests of the legal system. Like many feminists elsewhere, *Féministes Révolutionnaires* drew attention to the way in which the legal system put the victim rather than the rapist on trial. They saw rapists not as victims of capitalism, nor as individual criminals, but as 'the private militia of patriarchal justice' (rhodes and McNeil, 1985: 35–9).

Questions Féministes and Nouvelles Questions Féministes

One means of combating the effects of the fragmentation of the MLF was to set up publications which could reach an audience beyond those who belonged to small feminist groups or participated in specific campaigns. In 1977 some women who had been active in *Féministes Révolutionnaires* along with others who supported their political analysis, founded a new theoretical journal, *Questions Féministes*. This journal and its successor, *Nouvelles Questions Féministes*, became Delphy's central political project. The original collective which founded *Questions Féministes* included Delphy and Lesseps along with Colette Guillaumin, Nicole-Claude Mathieu and Monique Plaza. Simone de Beauvoir acted as titular editor, but played little part in the running of the journal. Monique Wittig, whose participation was later to prove critical, joined the collective about a year after the journal started publication. The first issue, in November 1977, contained a collectively written editorial entitled 'variations on a common theme' which outlined the founding principles of the journal and located its radical feminist perspective in relation to the two other major feminist tendencies in France. Their project, they said, 'was born from the recognition that feminism does not have its own space for theoretical debate' (*QF* Collective, [1977] 1981: 212). Feminists were at that time writing for a range of left and radical publications, and other new feminist publications were launched around the same time, such as *La Revue d'en Face*, but *Questions Féministes* made a unique contribution in devoting itself explicitly to radical feminist theory. In starting a theoretical journal, the collective were by no means distancing themselves from politics: they saw the production of theory as serving political ends. Theory was not, for them, something obscure, inaccessible and removed from experience – although they recognized that the term was often used to refer to 'inaccessible texts that are destined for a privileged social elite' (1981: 212). They sought to break the equation between theory and inaccessibility, 'to make theory everyone's concern, so that each of us can not only use it but also produce it' (1981: 213). Theory was to be redefined to serve feminism:

> We consider as theoretical *any discourse, whatever its language may be,* that attempts to *explain the causes and the mechanisms,* the *why* and the *how* of women's oppression. . . . 'Theoretical' means any discourse that attempts to draw political conclusions, that offers a strategy or tactics to the feminist movement. (1981: 213; emphasis in original)

Their purpose was to offer an arena for debate in order to bring into being feminist knowledge, a 'feminist science' which would challenge the patriarchal ideology that currently passes as 'scientific discourse'. This feminist science would 'account for hierarchical patriarchal structures' and provide strategies for subverting them, enabling feminists 'to intervene wherever the powers that be, whose direct aim is the reproduction of patriarchal structures, are in action' (1981: 214).

Feminism, for *Questions Féministes*, requires the analysis of both the material basis of women's oppression and the ideologies which reinforce and perpetuate it. Considerable space in 'variations on a common theme' was given over to a critique of what the collective call the 'neo-femininity' tendency in French theory which is associated with *Psych et Po* and others adopting a psychoanalytic perspective. The collective argue against those who propose a recovery of feminine 'difference', since they see this as playing into the hands of patriarchal ideology which defines women as 'different' in order to justify their subordination. Feminists associated with *Questions Féministes* always insisted that femininity is socially constructed and that 'men' and 'women' are social rather than natural categories. This is related to the fundamental tenet of French radical feminism – restated in the first *Questions Féministes* editorial – that the relationship between men and women is a class relationship and that the 'difference' between them is that between oppressor and oppressed. As well as distancing them from the 'neo-femininity' school, this also differentiates their position from that of socialist feminism, or the 'class struggle tendency'. The latter, they say, deal with women's oppression simply by adding it to existing marxist theory without questioning the primacy of working class struggle or the idea that the only system of oppression is capitalism. They therefore fail to address the gaps in marxist theory and tend to treat sexism as ideological and have no analysis of the material bases of women's oppression:

> One must study the connections between sexist mentality, institutions, laws, and the socio-economic structures which support them. These structures are part of a specific system different from the capitalist system and we call this system 'patriarchy'. (1981: 217)

Questions Féministes was thus dedicated to the analysis of patriarchy as a social system in which men and women constitute classes with opposing interests. While the collective agreed on these basic premises, it became clear within three years that they did not agree on the political consequences of their analysis. The journal lasted in its original form only until 1980, when the collective split in an acrimonious dispute over political or radical lesbianism and *Questions Féministes* ceased to exist. Delphy and Lesseps, who opposed the radical lesbian position, subsequently launched *Nouvelles Questions Féministes* amid public denunciations of them and legal action against them from their former colleagues. The original collective was formally dissolved in October 1980 and both sides signed an agreement that neither would use the title *Questions Féministes* for another journal. When the publication of *Nouvelles Questions Féministes* was announced, the other members of the *QF* collective demanded that the title should be withdrawn and subsequently contested the right to the title in court. Delphy's faction won the day, supported by Simone de Beauvoir, and *Nouvelles Questions Féministes* survived. The *NQF* collective were clearly in line with the technical terms of the agreement signed by the old *QF* collective, but there were many in the movement who felt that they had gone against its spirit. Equally, there were plenty of feminists who supported their stand against radical lesbianism (Duchen, 1984, 1986, 1987).

In order to explain how a group of feminists once united around a common cause found themselves in such a situation, it is necessary to outline the background to this dispute. The point of view of both sides is a matter of record. The *NQF* collective put their case in the first editorial of the new journal, while their erstwhile colleagues told their side of the story in a 'letter to the women's movement' distributed at a meeting on International Women's Day in 1981 (both reprinted in Duchen, 1987). The conflict over radical lesbianism was by no means confined to the *QF* collective – it divided radical feminists as a whole. Nor was this a peculiarly French issue, but was being debated in many Western countries. In Britain for example, a similarly heated controversy was sparked off by a paper on political lesbianism written by the Leeds Revolutionary Feminists (see Onlywomen Press, 1981). In other Western countries the divisions this issue engendered were already visible in the 1970s, but did not become widely apparent in France until 1980 – in part because such differences were submerged by the need to retain a united radical feminist front against *Psych et Po* (Duchen, 1984).

By early 1980 radical lesbians had become a visible tendency within France. Among them were those known as the Jussieu group, who were to become central actors in the conflict, and one of whom was a member of the *QF* collective.[8] In February 1980 *Questions Féministes* published two articles, each representing one side of the debate. The first of these was Monique Wittig's 'The straight mind', in which she challenged the heterosexual thinking she saw as underlying patriarchal culture. The category 'woman', she argued, had no meaning outside 'heterosexual systems of thought'. She concluded that, because they live outside heterosexuality, 'lesbians are not women' (Wittig, [1980] 1992: 32). The other article, 'Heterosexuality and Feminism' by Emmanuèle de Lesseps, was not a critique of Wittig's theoretical position, but of the politics of radical lesbianism in general. While acknowledging the contradictions heterosexual feminists face, Lesseps rejected the idea that all feminists should become lesbians or that feminism should exclude heterosexual women. This she saw as turning the feminist movement, which began from women's common experience, against women. The next issue of the journal published a further article by Wittig, 'One is not born a woman', in which she expanded on the argument that lesbians were fugitives from the class relations of heterosexuality. These articles served to define the two opposing factions, but conflicts within the collective did not centre on the articles as such and indeed Wittig herself appears to have played little personal part. From both the written accounts (Duchen, 1984, 1986) and from Delphy's memories of the events, it seems that the debate generated by the articles in the wider movement, and the resultant tensions, fed back into the collective. This was exacerbated by strains in personal relationships which already existed.

It is easier to grasp the political positions being advanced than to unravel the causes of the personal animosity the debate generated. Each side saw its position as deriving from the central tenet of radical feminism: that 'men' and 'women' are classes. As the radical lesbians from *QF* put it in their 'letter to the feminist movement', they were pushing 'the logic of radical feminist analysis to its logical conclusion' and identified with 'a lesbian political analysis which considers the *class of men* to be the main enemy' (in Duchen, 1987: 85; emphasis in original). If men are the class enemy, they argued, feminists should withdraw from any personal relationships with them, should refuse to service them sexually or otherwise, and should devote all their energies to the liberation of women. Radical lesbianism is thus not a question of sexual identity but of political commitment and is the only truly revolutionary stance for feminists to take. Lesbians within this current argued that heterosexuality was 'antagonistic to feminist commitment' (in Duchen, 1987: 85) and that those who did not see this were at best reformist and at worst class 'collaborators' (in Duchen, 1987: 87). The issue of heterosexual women's 'collaboration' was what transformed a political position into a potentially personal attack on other women (see also Duchen, 1984).

The editorial to the first issue of *Nouvelles Questions Féministes* counters these arguments, putting the case which Delphy and

Lesseps had argued throughout the dispute. They saw the political conclusions of the radical lesbians as 'incompatible with the principles of feminism and with the theoretical and political orientation of the journal' (in Duchen, 1987: 81). They go on:

> We believed this conclusion contradicted the premises of radical feminism: i.e. the recognition that women, all women, constitute an oppressed class; that we are all oppressed by men as a class; and that feminism is the struggle against this *common* oppression of women. The term 'collaborators' denotes political enemies, not those who share ones oppression, not allies. (in Duchen, 1987: 81–2; emphasis in original)

Those opposed to radical lesbianism saw the necessity of a critique of heterosexuality, but insisted that this should be dissociated from a 'condemnation of heterosexual women' (in Duchen, 1987: 82). They also questioned the implication that radical lesbians were a political vanguard, 'the most advanced feminists' (in Duchen, 1987: 82). They felt that the founding analysis of the *QF* collective, that women were a class, had been 'perverted' so that heterosexual feminists, rather than men, were now being defined as the enemy.

The dispute within the *QF* collective raged between March and June 1980, fuelled by the activities of the Jussieu lesbians. This group had organized a meeting at which heterosexual feminists had been called 'collaborators' and lesbians who supported them 'kapos' (prisoners in concentration camps who cooperated with the guards and were placed in authority over other prisoners). Within the *QF* collective, Delphy and Lesseps tried to raise questions about these charges of collaboration which implicitly or explicitly were made specifically against Lesseps. Lesseps understandably felt insulted and Delphy was outraged that an old friend and a good feminist should be subjected to such accusations.[9] Others in the collective defended the member who was in the Jussieu group, arguing that this was not the main point at issue, that the debate should be about the institution of heterosexuality. The editors of *Nouvelles Questions Féministes* saw this as 'intellectual terrorism', in that they were not allowed to criticize any aspect of the radical lesbian position without being seen as opposing all of it: 'If one criticizes the condemnation of heterosexual women, in their eyes that means one refuses to criticize heterosexuality' (in

Duchen, 1987: 82). With personal insults traded in both directions, it became evident that the collective could no longer work together.

In publishing *Nouvelles Questions Féministes*, Delphy wanted to continue the work of the original journal which had, as she saw it, been disrupted by the radical lesbians. This is made clear in the first editorial to the new journal: 'the change of title in no way indicates a change of direction or of content'. The founders of the new journal were Delphy, Lesseps, Beauvoir and Claude Hennequin, but Lesseps soon withdrew. Since then Delphy has been the sole individual, after the death of Beauvoir, to have been involved with it consistently. Others have come and gone and have included at various times Françoise Basch, Arlette Gautier, Kathleen Barry and Christiana Anglefors. By the mid-1990s a stable editorial team had been established consisting of Delphy with Françoise Armengaud, Ghaiss Jasser and Willemien Visser. As I write (in 1995) the journal has survived, with some breaks in publication, for 15 years. It continues to publish theoretical articles and to keep up with debates in the wider movement. In 1994 and 1995, for example, two special issues have dealt with the arguments for and against 'parity' in politics: whether or not women should seek to be represented in equal numbers with men in the French parliament.

Theory and scholarship

So far I have concentrated on Delphy's involvement in the French feminist movement and have said little about her academic career or the theoretical work which is the main focus of this book. During most of her academic career she has been elaborating her materialist feminist perspective and has written both polemical and more scholarly work on this theme. She has also since 1966 worked within the same organization, the Centre Nationale de Reserche Scientifique (CNRS), although she has been attached to various different sections of that organization at different times. CNRS is a French government organization devoted to scholarly research. Once past the most junior grades researchers are free to pursue their own interests, which has given Delphy the scope to devote her energy to feminist scholarship.

Delphy spent her first four years at CNRS as a research assistant, which meant that she worked primarily on other people's research and that any independent work she carried out had to be approved by her superiors. She was initially attached to the rural sociology group. It was in this period that she worked on patterns of inheritance in rural families (Delphy, 1969, 1976c). She had wanted to do research on women, but was not permitted to do so. She says: 'I chose to study the inheritance of property instead, hoping to get back to my original interest eventually, by an indirect route' (1984: 15). She came to see this experience as extremely valuable since it gave her an insight into the economic functioning of families which she drew on in developing her more specifically feminist analysis of patriarchal exploitation (see Chapters 3 and 4). In 1970 she was promoted to attaché de reserche (the equivalent of an untenured research fellow) and transferred to the sociological research group based at the University of Paris X, at Nanterre. She subsequently worked with Yves Dezalay conducting research on divorce and was able to secure the employment of Emmanuèle de Lesseps as a research assistant on this project (Delphy, 1974, 1976b). In 1977 she was again promoted, this time to a tenured position which gave her the freedom to pursue her own interests. By the end of the 1970s she had published a number of scholarly works on economic relations within families as well as several interventions into feminist debates. During the 1980s, under the socialist administration of Mitterrand, Women's Studies in France began to be given some resources. In 1983 a research group on Gender and Society was set up within the central social science section of CNRS which Delphy joined. This group was charged with overseeing government grants for research in women's studies and funded 80 projects. Since the Gender and Society group folded in 1989 she has remained at the same location, pursuing her own work. In recent years she has produced work on gender, motherhood and the legal position of women and children (Delphy, 1991a, 1991c, 1992, 1993a, 1993b, 1994), as well as commentaries on political events in France (Delphy, 1991b, 1995; Armengaud et al., 1995).[10]

Delphy's ideas have been known outside France for some time: her work began to reach an international audience by the late

1970s and has been translated into Italian, Spanish and German as well as English. The spread of Delphy's ideas within the English speaking world owes much to her collaboration with a British feminist, Diana Leonard. They met and became friends in the early 1970s and found much common ground between them. Both were sociologists interested in developing a feminist perspective on marriage and the family. Leonard found French materialist feminism useful in making sense of her own research on courtship and marriage (Leonard, 1980, 1990a) and saw its potential as a theoretical foundation for radical feminism. Since she was fluent in French and familiar with feminist debates within France, she was in a position to translate this work and to contextualize it for an English audience. Other translations of French materialist feminist writings exist. The American journal *Feminist Issues* was originally founded with the intention of bringing these ideas to a wider audience. After the split in the *QF* collective, however, they sided with the radical lesbians and ceased to include Delphy's articles, having published only two in the first annual volume in 1981 (1981a, 1981d). English speakers are therefore largely reliant on Leonard's translation (and often editorship) for access to Delphy's work.

Delphy and Leonard first met at an International Sociological Association conference on the family in 1972. Diana Leonard (then Barker) was one of the organizers of the 1974 British Sociological Association (BSA) conference, on the subject of Sexual Divisions and Society. The theme was inspired by the rise of the feminist and gay liberation movements and the conference was to prove important in establishing a specifically feminist agenda within British sociology (see Barker and Allen, 1976). Leonard invited Delphy and Dezalay to give a joint paper on their work on divorce, from which each produced a separate contribution to one of the books to emerge from the conference (Barker and Allen, 1976; Delphy, 1976b; Dezalay, 1976). Delphy's article 'Continuities and discontinuities in marriage and divorce' was thus the first she had published in English, although a mimeographed translation of 'The main enemy' had been in circulation within the women's movement since the 1974 Women's Liberation Conference.

During and after the BSA conference, Delphy and Leonard began to work closely together on two projects. The first was a joint book on women and the family originally intended as a short text for a women's studies series, but which emerged many years later as a much more substantial theoretical work: *Familiar Exploitation* (1992). A second, shorter term, project was to gain funding for a series of Anglo-French seminars. These seminars, bringing together feminist sociologists from France and Britain, took place over the years 1975 to 1977. The British participants varied but included, in addition to Diana Leonard, Leonore Davidoff, Mary McIntosh, Jean Gardiner, Maxine Molyneux and Anne Whitehead. These were all, with the exception of Leonard, marxist feminists while the French group were materialist radical feminists. The French participants remained constant: Christine Delphy, Nicole-Claude Mathieu, Noelle Bisseret, Monique Plaza, Emmanuèle de Lesseps and Colette Capitan-Peter – the women who were to found *Questions Féministes*. These seminars were crucial in bringing the founding *QF* collective together as well as providing a context in which Delphy and Leonard continued to collaborate and share ideas.

During this period Diana Leonard was also involved in the Women's Research and Resources Centre, founded in London in 1975, and in the publications collective that developed as part of the Centre's aim of promoting feminist research and theory. In 1977, as part of their 'Explorations in Feminism' series, they published two pamphlets featuring the work of French materialist feminists: Nicole-Claude Mathieu's *Ignored by Some Denied by Others: the Social Sex Category in Sociology* and Christine Delphy's *The Main Enemy*. The latter included not only the title essay, in its original translation by Lucy ap Roberts, but also two new translations by Diana Leonard – 'Proto-feminism and anti-feminism' and a debate between Delphy and Danièle Léger on domestic labour. Later, when the Explorations in Feminism collective went into partnership with the publishers Hutchinson, a much more substantial collection of Delphy's work was published under the title *Close to Home* (1984). Again this was edited by Leonard, who also translated the articles previously unavailable in English, and provided new and clearer translations of work which had already appeared in English.

Through Leonard, Delphy met Jalna Hanmer, an American (US)

radical feminist teaching at the University of Bradford, who invited her to spend a term there in 1979. During this period Delphy gave open seminars at Bradford and also participated in a radical feminist day school in London in April 1979. Here she gave a paper responding to her British marxist feminist critics, a version of which was subsequently published in *Feminist Review* (Delphy, 1980b). In 1982 Delphy and Leonard were invited as plenary speakers to the British Sociological Association annual conference, and gave a paper based on their collaborative work. The following year Hanmer, Leonard and others founded the radical feminist magazine *Trouble and Strife*, originally envisaged by them as giving a voice to a current in British radical feminism sharing similar views to those involved in *Nouvelles Questions Féministes*. This magazine covered the radical lesbianism debate in France (Duchen, 1984) and has since published some of Delphy's recent articles (Delphy, 1992; Armengaud et al., 1995).

Throughout the 1980s Delphy and Leonard continued to work closely together, with much mutual visiting between France and Britain. *Familiar Exploitation* is the product of nearly two decades' work, during which time each has exerted an influence on the other's ideas. The importance of Leonard's contribution to our understanding of Delphy's work should not be underestimated. It is not just the fact that most of Delphy's work in English is mediated through Leonard, but the quality of the translations themselves that matter. Translation is not a simple matter of transferring words from one language to another in a literal sense. A good translator needs to understand the work itself, the context in which it was produced and the audience it is being translated for. In the case of theoretical and political writings this means selecting concepts with appropriate resonance for those reading the work in a different cultural context, which make sense in terms of debates current among those readers. It may also mean restructuring sentences so that a complex argument retains its intelligibility. To make this point I will quote from alternative translations of Delphy's work. First, a passage from 'For a materialist feminism' as it appeared in *Feminist Issues*, in which Delphy is arguing that the construction of knowledge as distinct disciplines is an effect of ideology:

> The idea that there exist separate domains of experience, with which distinct disciplines occupy themselves, each having its own methods which are afterwards joined in order to juxtapose their 'findings', is typically antimaterialist. (1981a: 71)

The same passage as translated by Leonard becomes far less tortuous:

> The idea that there are separate areas of experience which are the concern of the different disciplines, each with its own methods, and that these can afterwards be joined so as to juxtapose their findings, is typically anti-materialist. (1984: 213)

Other examples could be given. The point is that Leonard's intimate knowledge of Delphy's work enables her to produce translations which make good sense to English readers.

In the remainder of this book I will offer an overview of both Delphy's individual work and her joint work with Leonard. I will begin by discussing the basic premises of materialist feminism and then go on to consider central areas of Delphy's work. In so doing I will aim to contextualize her ideas in two ways. First, to locate them within the tradition of French materialist feminism within which they were produced, and second, to relate them to wider developments in feminist theory.

Notes

1. My source here is an interview conducted with Delphy in August 1993. Unless other sources are cited, all statements and views attributed to Delphy in this chapter are based upon this interview.

2. There is some discrepancy in the dates of origin attributed to this group. The date I have given is Delphy's (1991b), which is based upon what she was told of this group by Gille and Monique Wittig. Antionette Fouque, in an interview in *Le Matin* in 1980 (reprinted in Duchen, 1987), says that she and two other women started meeting in October 1968 and claims that this – rather than the events of 1970 – was 'the real genesis of the movement' (Fouque, 1987: 51). Marks and Courtivron (1981) and Kaplan (1992) compound the confusion by stating that *Psych et Po* originated in 1968. Fouque's group, by her own account, had no name at this point and only became known as *Psych et Po* in the early 1970s, after the radical feminists had left it.

3. It was originally entitled 'Pour un mouvement de libération des femmes' (for a women's liberation movement), but was retitled by the editors, using the form 'la femme' or 'woman' – a term consistently employed by the press to the annoyance of feminists.

4. Wittig may have already had a more public reputation, since she had published her first novel, *Les guérillères*, the previous year. She was to become a feminist writer of world renown.

5. Although 'féministes révolutionnaires' translates literally as 'revolutionary feminists', their position was closer to that of radical feminists in Britain and the USA than to revolutionary feminists in Britain. I have, accordingly characterized them as radical feminists, which is Delphy's own preferred term.

6. Along with her partner, Jean-Paul Sartre, Beauvoir was enough of a public figure to be relatively immune from government harassment and prosecution. Both used this immunity in the service of progressive causes. In particular they often took on titular editorships of left papers, without wishing to exercise editorial control, in order to protect their publishers from prosecution and legal action.

7. As published in *Le Nouvel Observateur*, 5 April 1971. My wording is based on three translations, those of Duchen (1986: 12), Tristan and Pisan (1987: 48), and Marks and Courtivron (1981: 190).

8. In the written sources on the *QF* split, particular protagonists are not identified by name except where they had given their views in print, although those who knew the individuals involved can identify who is who from the accounts. Delphy has given me details of who stood where in this controversy, but I have refrained from naming individuals except where this is unavoidable. My own account is based primarily on the written sources supplemented by what Delphy has told me. I will endeavour to make clear the points that derive from Delphy's own memory of these events.

9. From my interview with Delphy, August 1993.

10. For details of these articles, see the annotated bibliography at the end of this volume.

2

Delphy's Materialist Feminism

According to Simone de Beauvoir, feminist theory in France 'has emanated almost exclusively from radical feminists' (Beauvoir, 1985: 236). Feminists from other countries might find this assertion rather strange. What, they might ask, happened to socialist or marxist feminist theory? It is true that socialist feminists have always been visible and vocal participants in the grass-roots movement in France, but compared with their counterparts elsewhere in the West, they have generated little theory. There is a second, and more important, reason why some might question Beauvoir's emphasis on radical feminism. This is because there is something else called 'French feminist theory' which bears no resemblance to radical feminism – some might argue to any form of feminism (Delphy, 1995).

The term 'French feminism' has come to denote something quite different from feminism in France. 'French feminism' is largely an Anglo-American invention which canonizes some French theorists while completely ignoring others. Within France, those engaged in psychoanalytic theorizing about femininity, exploring women's relationships to their body and 'feminine' language, have not generally defined themselves as feminists. Yet this is what is identified as 'French feminism' outside France. The 'holy trinity' of women theorists are Héléne Cixous, Julia Kristeva and Luce Irigaray (Landry and MacLean, 1993: 54). The relationship of these theorists with the women's movement in France is ambiguous and ambivalent; of the three only Irigaray has ever identified as a feminist. All three have at some time been connected, if only fleetingly, with *Psych et Po* (Moi, 1987), an organization which declares itself anti-feminist and whose relationship with the MLF has been highly problematic (see Chapter 1). 'French feminism' can also mean feminist work which draws on the work of certain male French theorists, particularly that of another trinity: Lacan, Foucault and Derrida. All of these theorists, male and female, are sometimes grouped together under another Anglo-American label: postmodernism.

This misrepresentation can be seen in most anthologies of work by or about 'French feminists' (for example Fraser and Bartky, 1992; Jardine and Smith, 1987; Marks and Courtivron, 1981). It is particularly prevalent in works on literary criticism, where this brand of theory has been most influential and through which it has been promoted within English speaking countries (see, for example Jardine, 1985; Moi, 1985). The boundaries of 'French feminism' are thus strangely constructed to exclude most feminists in France while including some male theorists and sometimes even anglophone theorists who cite the appropriate French authors. Women who do not call themselves feminists fall within its definition, those who have always called themselves feminists do not.

The impression of French feminism derived from this construction is that it is concerned largely with questions of language and psychoanalysis. This has the effect of defining other forms of feminism out of existence. In the introduction to her edited collection *French Feminist Thought*, Toril Moi explains this in terms of the relative similarity between these excluded feminists and English-speaking feminists: that they are doing work which we in Britain or North America or Australia would recognize as feminist, and share our preoccupations with 'the historical and social reality of women's experience'. They are thus ignored because they are 'perceived as lacking in exotic difference' (Moi, 1987: 6). Yet Moi herself bears some responsibility for this exclusion. In the same introduction she names as the 'three major French feminist theorists of the 1970s', Cixous, Irigaray and Kristeva (1987: 4), and in her earlier work she sets up an opposition between 'French' and 'Anglo-American' feminist criticism (Moi, 1985). French radical feminism, in particular, suffers from this silencing. The sole representative of this perspective ever included within 'French feminism' is Wittig, but she is generally read in conjunction with the 'trinity' rather than as a radical feminist and her work suffers misrepresentation as a result (see Chapter 5). Sometimes French radical feminism is reinvented. Chris Weedon even goes so far as to identify the 'trinity', and Irigaray in particular, with radical feminism, completely ignoring those in France who call themselves radical feminists (Weedon, 1987: 9). In part this is to do with Weedon's misrepresentation of radical feminism as essentialist or at least as asserting women's essential 'difference'. The real radical feminists in France – those who so name themselves – have always vigorously opposed this point of view. For example, much of the editorial of the first issue of their journal *Questions Féministes* was devoted to a polemic against this doctrine of 'neo-femininity'.

Delphy herself has recently gone on record to combat this Anglo-American representation of French feminism. In an article published in *Yale French Studies* (Delphy, 1995), she suggests that it is a form of imperialism whereby women from another country are denied the right to speak for themselves. She asks how American women would feel if an unrepresentative handful of individuals were defined in France as constituting 'American feminism', for example, if Camille Paglia was elevated to a status in France comparable with that occupied by Julia Kristeva in the USA. She also makes the point that the women identified as 'French feminists' outside France are not only marginal to the women's movement in her country but also to academic feminist theory and Women's Studies. As an example she talks about the proposals submitted to the Gender and Society research group of the CNRS in the years 1983–9 (see Chapter 1). Over this period the board of the research programme considered over 300 applications from all disciplines, including literary criticism, and funded 80 of them. What is striking about these proposals is the absence from their bibliographies of the individuals singled out as important feminist theorists by British and American writers. In France these theorists have nothing like the influence attributed to them by outsiders (Delphy, 1995).

Within France, then, radical feminist theory has been far more significant than is generally recognized and materialist radical feminism has been particularly prominent. Wittig (1992) credits Christine Delphy with the invention of the term materialist feminism, although she was not its sole exponent. Apart from Delphy and Wittig, others who contributed to the development of this perspective and who were associated with the journal *Questions Féministes* are little known outside France. Ignorance of this tendency often means that both Delphy and Wittig are frequently treated as if they were isolated exponents of their theories. Moreover, further misunderstandings arise because there are other forms of feminism labelled materialist. Since the existence of diverse feminisms claiming the title 'materialist' can be confusing, I will briefly consider how these differ from French materialist feminism.

One form of 'materialism' accounts for women's subordination in terms of their relationship to reproduction or their relationship to their bodies. One of the best known exponents of this perspective is Mary O'Brien (1981), who argues that masculine theory and male domination stem from men's specific and alienated relationship to reproduction. O'Brien does engage with Marx, but her analysis is materialist in the philosophical rather than marxist sense: a perspective which asserts the primacy of matter over mind, the matter in question being the body. This perspective does at least have a known philosophical tradition behind it and therefore some claim to the term 'materialist'. It is, however, very different from the historical materialism developed by Marx and endorsed by French materialist feminists: the latter accords historical, social conditions priority over nature, arguing that human activity transforms nature and that we are social, not natural, beings.

More recently the term materialist feminism has been reinvented by theorists arguing from a very different perspective, particularly in books by Donna Landry and Gerald MacLean (1993) and Rosemary Hennessy (1993). Both texts claim some marxist antecedents, but their main intellectual influence is that body of theory known as 'postmodernism'. For both their 'materialism' is motivated by wish to avoid some of the political consequences associated with postmodernism, particularly its potential to deny the existence of any material reality outside language and discourse. Those now claiming the name 'materialist' have become aware that this severely handicaps any radical social critique since it implies that, say, patriarchy or racism are purely discursive constructs with no foundation in material social conditions. Hence Hennessy argues that materialist feminism needs to retain 'its critique of social totalities like patriarchy and capitalism' (1993: xii). Both Hennessy and Landry and MacLean seem to be only dimly aware of what materialist feminism has been – they conflate it with marxist feminism even while claiming they do not. Landry and MacLean are critical of the construction of French feminism which ignores French materialist feminism (1993: 54–5), but proceed to ignore it themselves apart from passing references to Delphy and Wittig. Hennessy cites Delphy among others she sees as having contributed to the early development of materialist feminism – a list mainly comprising marxist feminist opponents of materialist feminism (1993: xi) – and gives some cursory consideration to Wittig. Neither text shows any understanding of what makes a materialist feminist analysis materialist, nor how it differs from marxist or socialist feminism. In both cases what is being identified as materialist feminism is a form of (post)marxism infused with postmodernism. Indeed Hennessy comes close to defining it in this way: 'Materialist feminism is distinguished from socialist feminism in part because it embraces postmodern conceptions of language and subjectivity' (1993: 5). These texts render French materialist feminism virtually invisible.

What is materialism?

The materialism of French radical feminists derived from marxism although they were highly critical of the form of marxism which subordinates women's liberation to the 'class struggle'. The term 'materialism', or more specifically 'historical materialism', was first coined by Karl Marx to describe his method of social analysis. It is because this method was developed in order to understand systems of oppression and exploitation that it is potentially useful to feminists; and it is the method, rather than the specific content, of his analysis that appealed to French radical feminists. Marx himself, of course, dealt primarily with class, not gender, inequality. Where marxist feminists tried to fit gender inequality into Marx's existing analysis of the class structure, materialist radical feminists instead applied Marx's method to the analysis of patriarchy. This is what makes their position radical feminist and, from the point of view of conventional marxists, heretical. Much of the early criticism of Delphy's work consisted of demonstrating that she was not properly marxist, that she paid insufficient attention to the chapter and verse of Marx's writings (see Chapter 3). Delphy's rejection of this 'biblical' approach to Marx is not intended as a dismissal of his analysis of the class relations of capitalism. Rather, she argues that patriarchy needs to be understood as a system of domination and exploitation in its own right, not simply fitted into a theory of class exploitation (Delphy, 1980b, 1980c).

Delphy has suggested that materialism is best understood in terms of what it stands against,[1] and this is perhaps the simplest way to proceed. When first used by Marx, it was indeed employed in contradistinction to another perspective, idealism – the notion that ideas constitute the motor of historical change and determine social and cultural life. As a consequence of anti-idealism, historical materialism also stands opposed to what we might call psychologism and biologism. I will expand on each of these points in turn, applying them to the issue of gender inequality, in order to explain not only what materialism stands against, but also what it stands for.

Materialism is anti-idealist in that ideas in themselves cannot be seen as the cause of any form of social division or oppression. On the contrary, inequalities are rooted in actual social practices, the day-to-day way in which we conduct our lives. This does not mean that ideas are irrelevant. When they become woven into ideology they can serve to conceal inequalities or to justify existing social arrangements as natural. Ideology then becomes embedded in the social practices it legitimizes. For example, the fact that in most heterosexual couples women do the bulk of the housework is a social practice with material effects – that women work for men and men benefit from having this work done for them. Ideas such as 'a woman's place is in the home' or 'housework is a labour of love' are part of an ideology which justifies this division of labour as natural, which hides the oppression it entails and helps to perpetuate it. Women may accept their unfair domestic burden because they believe it is their 'natural' lot or in order to demonstrate that they care for their husbands. But this is not the only reason for their compliance. They are also tied into this situation by other material factors, importantly their economic dependence on their husbands' higher wages which in turn derives from gender inequality in the labour market. Inequality in the labour market is further reinforced by the material fact that women's responsibility for childcare and housework restricts their employment opportunities. It is also justified by the idea – itself rooted in material practices – that because women are economic dependants they do not 'need' decent wages. In materialist analysis, then, ideology is never considered in isolation from the social structures and practices in which it is rooted. This distinguishes materialist feminism from those analyses which claim that gender inequality is primarily ideological or (in more recent work) that it is the product of 'discourse' – the ways in which we think about, make sense of, the social world. It is not ideas about women and men that create inequality between them, but material inequality which gives rise to certain ideas about women and men.

A corollary of anti-idealism is anti-psychologism. Materialism is opposed to the notion that inequality derives from, or is perpetuated primarily at the level of, our individual psyches, what goes on in our heads. Rather, what goes on in our heads is thought of as deriving from our material situation, as in Marx's dictum that 'life is not determined by consciousness, but consciousness by life'. Hence it is not psychological differences between women and men that cause the inequality between them, rather that inequality itself has psychological consequences. This does not mean that subjectivity – our sense of ourselves, our feelings, desires, attitudes and aptitudes – is irrelevant. Again this may help to sustain and stabilize current social practices. Here ideology and subjectivity are linked. Ideology works, is effective, because it becomes part of us, part of how we think and feel. To go back to the situation of the housewife, she cares for her husband and defers to his needs not merely from a sense of duty, but because being caring, nurturant and deferential is part of being feminine within our society. Her husband may expect to be serviced and deferred to, and may become unpleasant or even violent if these expectations are not met, because being dominant and aggressive is part of being masculine (within our society). However, these qualities are not absolutely intrinsic to the psyches of this ideal typical couple – they are also rooted in social practices and relationships, particularly material power differences. The authoritarian husband is far less likely to exhibit dominance and aggression towards his boss at work, the deferential wife may expect her young children to obey her.

The third feature of materialism is that it is anti-biologistic, anti-naturalistic, and anti-essentialist. In other words it is opposed to explanations rooted in biology, 'nature', or notions of essential, pre-given masculinity or femininity. Where ideological and psychological factors may play some part in a materialist analysis, little credence is given to biological arguments. Neither the hierarchy between the sexes nor the differences between them are seen as natural. Rather, gender divisions and gender hierarchy are social products. Hence the nurturant, deferential, feminine wife and the dominant, aggressive, masculine husband I have portrayed above were not born with these characteristics, but acquired them through living in a patriarchal society. Once again, then, materialism gives priority to the social. This is particularly true for the form of materialism I am dealing with here since, as I explained in the previous chapter, it developed its rigorous anti-essentialism in opposition to the 'neo-femininity' current in France.

Delphy and her colleagues have argued against the notion that women's difference can be the starting point of their liberation, that there is some essence of femininity repressed by patriarchy or that women can create a new language on the basis of their relationship to their bodies (*QF* collective, [1977] 1981). Since their radical feminism starts from the assumption that men and women are social groups, there can be no concept of 'woman' unrelated to social context. Nor can there be any direct relationship with our bodies capable of expression through a unique 'women's language', for this claim denies 'the reality and strength of social mediations' (1981: 219). There is no essential femininity, in language, in the body, or anywhere else, because femininity is socially defined. They oppose any perspective which rests on assumptions about nature since the 'one natural characteristic of human beings is that human beings are by nature social beings' (1981: 219). Men and women are what they are today because of the social relationships between them and it is these social relations which feminists should struggle to transform: 'The battle of the sexes is not biological' (1981: 223).

Materialist feminism, then, privileges the realm of social practices over ideology, psychology and biology; it looks for social causes of male dominance rather than ideological, psychological or biological causes. Importantly, this method of analysis involves a notion of social structure – institutionalized sets of social arrangements which pre-exist us as individuals. We are born into a particular place in a particular society and this imposes constraints on our lives, although we can and do resist these constraints and as feminists we struggle to change them. Economic inequality, and the exploitation it involves, is a fundamental aspect of the social and central to materialist analysis. This has been the focus of much of Delphy's work. Materialism is not, however, only concerned with the economic, but with material social practices and structures in general. Indeed materialists are careful not to reify the economy, not to see it as a 'thing' with an existence of its own, but rather as a realm of social relations, constructed through social activity (Delphy and Leonard, 1992).

One way of illustrating further what is involved in materialist feminism and how it differs from idealist and essentialist explanations of women's subordination is to look at a specific materialist critique. Delphy's acerbic review of Annie Leclerc's book *Parole de femme* ('woman's word' or the 'word of a woman') gives us a very clear picture of the differences between materialist feminists and what they call the 'neo-femininity' school. In particular, Delphy here focuses on the interconnections between idealism, biologism and psychologism.

Delphy versus Leclerc

Parole de femme was published in France in 1974 and received favourable reviews in the mainstream press. Leclerc contends that women have been devalued within masculine culture and silenced by masculine language. She posits the need for a woman's language derived from women's bodily experience and capable of representing the specificity of that experience.[2] Leclerc was not alone in arguing from the point of view of women's 'difference', nor was Delphy the only materialist feminist to criticize such writings.[3] It was precisely because *Parole de femme* was part of a wider trend in French thinking that Delphy felt it was important to refute its arguments. Leclerc stands for everything which materialist feminism stands against: 'Her whole system of thought rests on idealism and its variants, naturalism and biologism' (Delphy, [1976a] 1984: 183).

Delphy sees Leclerc's position as proto-feminist in that 'it is situated in the very first moments of individual revolt . . . prior to collective action' (1984: 182). Leclerc questions women's inferiority, but slides from proto-feminism to anti-feminism because she 'stays on men's terrain', premising her arguments on 'the dominant ideology' (1984: 183). First, she treats women and men as natural entities and takes the division of labour between them as given, indeed as 'judicious and rational' (quoted in Delphy, 1984: 183). Thus she accepts much of the dominant sexist ideology. Second, she accounts for women's subordination in an idealist fashion and thus assumes that 'it is values which determine social organization, not vice-versa' (Delphy, 1984: 183). For Leclerc it is men's values which enable them to glorify themselves and subjugate women.

Delphy sees Leclerc's biologism as leading inevitably to idealism. If cultural and social distinctions between women and men are taken as natural, only their evaluation can be questioned. Hence Leclerc can challenge male dominance only at the level of ideas. This conjunction of biologism and idealism is, Delphy argues, tautologous: women are devalued because they do women's work and women's work is devalued. Since this work is natural to women, this is tantamount to saying that 'the devaluation of being a woman derives from the devaluation of being a woman' (1984: 184).

According to Leclerc, women's claimed inferiority would be inconceivable if their domestic tasks 'were not considered as worthless, dirty or demeaning by men' (quoted in Delphy, 1994: 184). Thus domestic work is not seen as oppressive in itself, merely undervalued. How, Delphy asks, can men be in a position to impose their evaluation without being in a dominant position in the first place? Leclerc's argument inverts the causal logic of materialism, seeing the concrete disadvantages women suffer as the result of the ideological evaluation, rather than the evaluation as itself arising from material oppression. This is evident in the following passage quoted by Delphy:

> One would not know how to set about destroying the idea of the woman's inferiority or the fact of her exploitation if one did not also, and *particularly*, tackle the scorn, contempt or pity for the condition of women, whether it be biological (e.g. periods, childbirth) or traditional (e.g. domestic duties). (Leclerc in Delphy, 1984: 185; Delphy's emphasis)

Here, as Delphy says, it is unclear what Leclerc means by exploitation. Is Leclerc saying that exploitation consists simply of the unfair devaluation of women? How, Delphy inquires, can she 'rebel simultaneously against "the *miserable lot* of the woman" and against the fact that it is *unfairly considered* miserable?' (1984: 185; Delphy's emphasis). From Delphy's point of view, this contradiction arises from fundamentally flawed assumptions:

> Idealism has led Leclerc into an analytical blind alley: into taking the effect (the devaluation) for the cause (exploitation); and into a political blind alley: the analysis implies that we must change *not the reality of women's lives but the subjective evaluation of this reality.* She neither describes nor discusses the real –material – exploitation of women. (Delphy, 1984: 185; Delphy's emphasis)

Whatever Leclerc means by exploitation, she certainly does not think of it in terms of the material benefits which men receive from women's work: the foundation of Delphy's own analysis of patriarchal exploitation (see Chapter 3). This is clear in Leclerc's consideration of the benefits men derive from women's subordination. Here she argues that women are not primarily exploited but oppressed, in that men demand respect from them. She sees this as quite different from what is appropriated from other oppressed groups, such as slaves. Delphy sees this distinction between women's oppression and other forms of oppression as arbitrary. All oppression, she argues, produces a psychological benefit, respect, for the oppressors, but this is only one benefit among others. She maintains that it is particularly characteristic of relations of personal dependence – like slavery, serfdom and marriage – rather than the impersonal exploitation of capitalist relations. In such situations respect may be important in masking the extortion of services from the oppressed, as well as being a reward in itself. Leclerc, on the other hand, sees respect as the most important benefit accruing to men and material benefits as mere 'by-products' of it (Delphy, 1984: 187). Here Delphy identifies another incarnation of idealism at work: psychologism.

For Leclerc, the work women do for men is incidental: even if a man sometimes makes a woman 'sweat blood and kill herself with work', this is 'not at all determining' (Leclerc, in Delphy, 1984: 187). Delphy charges Leclerc with arguing a variant of the old idea that housework is a labour of love, ignoring the fact that this is how many women earn their living. Leclerc's account implies that 'it is but a statistical accident, a fortuitous coincidence, that all women have chosen to prove their love in the same way at the same time' (Delphy, 1984: 187). In setting up 'respect' as the main benefit men gain from women's subordination 'material oppression is automatically excluded as a motive and benefit' (Delphy, 1984: 197). Leclerc says: 'It is necessary that domestic work should be seen as lowly, humble . . . it is even necessary for the woman to suffer so as to bear witness of her respect' (in Delphy, 1984: 187). Delphy comments:

> The loop is looped. What women suffer is not due to their exploitation; on the contrary, their exploitation derives from their suffering. It is but a means to make them suffer. And to make them suffer is not even the objective: suffering itself is but a means to prove devotion . . . and it is pure chance if in the course of suffering women perform certain work from which men profit, again by chance. They would be equally happy if women could suffer while doing nothing. (Delphy, 1984: 187–8)

Leclerc's argument relies heavily on psychoanalysis, which Delphy calls 'the triumphant psychologism of the twentieth century', and in so doing 'unites psychologism and biologism' (Delphy,

1984: 188). Delphy's opposition to psychoanalysis, as she explains elsewhere (Delphy, 1975, 1981a, 1981b), does not derive from a lack of interest in subjectivity. Rather, she is suspicious of psychoanalysis because it explains social phenomena such as the relations between the sexes in terms of our inner psychic processes; this is why she sees it as psychologistic. Moreover, it divorces subjective, psychological processes from their material social context and is therefore idealist. Finally, it traces these psychic processes back to human anatomy and is therefore biologistic. This is precisely what happens in Leclerc's account. She reproduces the dominant ideology which says that divisions of labour between women and men result from their different procreative functions. Here Delphy sees biologism as a necessary prop for idealism. Because Leclerc thinks that the problem is the lowly value given to women, she refuses to consider the material foundations of that evaluation, the real power that men have over women; and since idealism asserts that values determine social organization, the 'origin of these values must therefore be sought *outside* society' (Delphy, 1984: 188; emphasis in original). Biology is one source of such extra-social explanations.

In searching for the source of the masculine values which lead men to derogate women, Leclerc looks to biology: these values reside in men's mode of ejaculation and she calls them 'death values'. Women, on the other hand, embody an opposing set of 'life values' rooted in their capacity to give birth. What Leclerc is doing here is to invert the dominant ideology which asserts masculine superiority: women are the natural repository of positive, life affirming values while men seek to impose their negative, death values: 'To attribute as she does a "death value" to ejaculation is to return the ideology of "A woman is determined by her uterus" to its sender: "A man is determined by his ejaculation"' (Delphy, 1984: 192). Delphy recognizes the appeal of this strategy, but regards it as flawed. It is one thing to have fun at men's expense by this reversal of patriarchal ideology, but it is dangerous to believe that in so doing you have discovered the ultimate weapon, since 'just as you turn the weapon on him, so the enemy can turn it back again' (Delphy, 1984: 190). She argues that inverting the conclusion of the dominant ideology in this way does not destroy that ideology, nor does it produce a counter ideology but rather another version of the same ideology. In order to demolish the dominant ideology we need to expose it *as* ideology, to demonstrate that it is both false and useful to the system. To do this requires a non-idealist, materialist explanation of women's oppression. Only by relating negative images of women to the oppression which produces them, and which they serve to justify, can we acquire a more positive image of ourselves as women. Leclerc's error, in Delphy's eyes, is that she tries to revalue femininity without confronting the material bases of women's oppression and never questions the naturalness of sexual divisions. Instead she simply offers her version of 'nature' in place of the patriarchal one.

For Delphy, then, it is as erroneous to reduce masculinity to men's ejaculation as it is to reduce femininity to women's procreative functioning. It 'involves an unscrupulous indulgence in a few sophisms which derive directly from magical thinking' (Delphy, 1984: 191). Delphy outlines the specious logic on which this argument depends as follows. It moves directly from physical sexual differences to presumed (but by no means proven) psychological differences between the sexes. It assumes the impossible: 'the replication of physiological mechanisms at the psychological level' (1984: 191). It accounts for the functioning of the whole person on the basis of certain of his or her cells. It completely ignores consciousness at the psychological level (we are mindlessly determined by our bodies) but at the same time imputes consciousness to physiological processes (ejaculation and childbirth are sources of particular values). We ought, says Delphy, to recognize the fallacy of such arguments because they have so often been used against us. For example, feminine passivity has been inferred from the imputed passivity of the ovum as opposed to the 'active' sperm. When women use this same sophistry against men, it remains just as invalid and does not advance our cause.

Even if Leclerc's account of the origins of men's values were not fallacious, it would still not explain how they were able to impose those values on women. It is not simply the way in which she accounts for masculine values which Delphy is critical of, but the way in which she attempts to base a causal explanation for women's oppression on these values. This idealism also undermines her attempt to counter the devaluation of women's biological condition. Delphy argues that we cannot recover a positive image of ourselves simply by revaluing our procreative functions, but must also develop means of defining ourselves other than by these functions. In other words we should resist ideological definitions of womanhood which reduce us to walking wombs:

> While Leclerc's book strives to revalue women's procreative functions, it also strives to imprison us in them: to reduce our being, our pleasures, our value . . . to them. In short she continues to define women in the same way as men (and the general ideology) do: by their relationship to men, and more particularly by their usefulness to men. Our use lies in our ability to bring into the world the only thing men cannot make. (1984: 193–4)

Delphy agrees that we need to revalue our bodies, our physical way of being in the world, but only as part of a wider feminist agenda. We cannot confine ourselves to the level of values nor to the level of our bodies. Where Delphy differs further from Leclerc is that she refuses to consider bodily attributes and functions as meaningful in themselves: 'the meaning of periods, for instance, is not given by the flow of blood, but, like all *meaning*, by consciousness, and thus by society' (1984: 194; Delphy's emphasis). Not only are the meanings given to physical events social in origin, but social constraints affect our experience of them. Hence cultural taboos surrounding menstruation shape its meaning, but so too does the lack of towels, tampons and disposal facilities in many public toilets. We cannot simply revalue menstruation or childbirth as 'natural', good, events as Leclerc would have us do without tackling the material conditions under which we menstruate or give birth.

It is not only women's bodies which Leclerc sees as lowly valued, but also the work they do. She assumes a natural division of labour which she projects back to the dawn of human pre-history. Leclerc is not alone in seeking the origins of women's oppression in the imagined conditions of our primordial forebears. Delphy is critical of such reconstructions because they inevitably project the present on to the past and invent a version of the past which fits with the author's preconceptions (see also Delphy, 1992, 1994). Leclerc assumes, as do many others, that a 'natural' division of labour was the consequence of women's childbearing. She recycles what Delphy calls our 'collective fantasies' about primitive societies: that all women were more or less permanently incapacitated by motherhood and relied on men to support them. She thus ignores the weight of anthropological evidence which shows that the work women actually do varies enormously from one society to another, and that women in most hunter-gatherer societies (those most like our prehistoric ancestors) are in fact major food providers. The myth of the primordial male provider, Delphy argues, is simply a way of making a social division appear natural and inevitable, thus legitimizing women's subordination.

Because Leclerc sees women's work as part of their natural condition, she seeks to revalue this work without asking anything about the social relations within which it is undertaken. From a materialist perspective it is these social relations which are all important.

> When Annie Leclerc says 'I don't ask why this lot has been given to women, but why this lot has been judged inferior', she is way off course. She cannot reply to the second question without asking the first; and if she doesn't ask the first question it is because, like many others, she wonders why the job is devalued but considers only the task. She evades the crucial intermediary variable: the fact that the job is defined not only by the task, but also and above all by the relations of production. It is work done in a subordinate relationship, and not the task, which is devalued. (Delphy, 1984: 206)[4]

For Delphy, women's oppression is not primarily a matter of values, but of real, material inequalities. Leclerc, on the other hand sees the revaluation of women's work and women's bodies as her central priority. Her recipe for remedying women's oppression, and indeed for curing all the ills of the world, is to achieve a balance between feminine and masculine values. These values are treated as if they are intrinsic to two pre-existing groups: women and men. She endorses the myth of complementarity between women and men, neglecting the hierarchy between them. Delphy, however, sees this hierarchy as producing divisions: masculine and feminine values do not reside in biological men and women but are the values of dominant and dominated groups. This is a theme she has returned to in recent work and she continues to critique those forms of feminism based on the assumption of women's difference (see Chapter 5).

The premises of Delphy's materialist feminism

In the final section of this chapter I will outline some of the key elements of Delphy's perspective, identifying themes which will be further developed in subsequent chapters, and I begin by saying a little more about her materialist method.

Delphy was attracted to Marx 's writings because of his emphasis on oppression and because his analysis of capitalism was motivated by a political commitment to freeing the working class from that oppression. This is what she sees as important in Marx. She is very opposed to those marxists who have set Marx's work up as a body of received wisdom that cannot be changed to accommodate forms of oppression other than that of the proletariat. She sees this as antithetical to the spirit of Marx's own writings: Marx himself did not try to fit the facts of an oppressive system into a pre-existing theory, instead he developed the theory to explain the oppression. This is how she thinks feminism should proceed, not by trying to fit women into Marx's analysis of capitalism but by extending and modifying Marx's materialist analysis to make sense of women's oppression (1975, 1980b). This is connected with another aspect of her method, arguing from the general to the particular. Rather than looking for what is specific to women's oppression and then trying to find explanations for it we should instead treat it as an instance of a wider phenomenon: the oppression of one group by another. Only then should we focus down on what is specific to women's oppression (Delphy, 1984; Delphy and Leonard, 1992).

She distrusts explanations which look only at what is specific to women because they so often came up with essentialist conclusions. For example, taking women's responsibility for childcare as part of their specific situation tends to lead to arguments that women are oppressed because they have babies. If, on the other hand, we start from the fact of oppression, we are more likely to see women's responsibility for childcare as a consequence, rather than a cause, of that oppression. A further, and perhaps more important, reason why Delphy dislikes explanations which overemphasize what is specific to women is that they are often associated with attempts to provide a total explanation of women's subordination, to isolate *the* cause or origins of it. This again tends to lead to essentialist arguments. Delphy does not believe that it is possible to provide a total theory of women's subordination. She sees this subordination as systematic, but not as being grounded in only one system. For example, she identifies the domestic mode of production as one such system, but points out this only explains one aspect of women's oppression: the exploitation of their domestic labour. She suggests that we need to explore other systems, other sets of social relations, through which women are subordinated and establish their interconnections with each other. She envisages these various systems as overlapping circles, in which case 'gender division is the zone illuminated by the projection of these circles on one another' (Delphy, 1984: 26). We have, she argues, barely made a start on delineating these various systems. We are as yet still a long way from fully understanding all aspects of women's oppression and even further from understanding how women's oppression intersects with other oppressions.

Those marxist feminists who adopt the concept of patriarchy often argue that it is ideological or rooted in relations of reproduction, thus retreating from materialism to idealist and biologistic arguments (see Delphy, 1981a, 1984).[5] Delphy, however, insists on a materialist analysis of patriarchy as well as of capitalism. Moreover, she chooses to focus on patriarchy, rather than trying to explore the interconnections between patriarchy and capitalism. This differentiates her from some others who advance a materialist analysis of patriarchy – such as the American marxist feminist Heidi Hartmann (1981) and the British materialist feminist Sylvia Walby (1986a). Whereas these theorists believe that we can only understand the development of patriarchy by analysing its articulation with capitalism, Delphy feels that we should find out more about patriarchy per se before we can understand how it is related to other systems. She sees herself as contributing to this gradual accumulation of knowledge.

It should be clear from what I have said about Delphy's distrust of total explanations that she does not see patriarchy as a monolithic, transhistorical phenomenon. While patriarchy refers to the systematic subordination of women, it is not itself a single system and it is certainly not something fixed and unchanging. Delphy is critical of theorists who use the term patriarchy to talk about an abstract system of male domination which has existed since the dawn of time. What she is interested in is patriarchal domination here and now: 'What I study is not an ahistoric entity which has wandered down through the centuries, but something peculiar to contemporary industrial societies' (Delphy, 1984: 17). She sees the search for the historical origins of women's oppression as fruitless and pointless and also ahistorical in that it denies what is specific to each historical period.

The central aspects of Delphy's analysis of patriarchy which I have identified in the chapters which follow are her analysis of familial relationships, her work on class and her development of the concept of gender. It is her work on families which is best known and which established her reputation as a theorist in the 1970s. In particular, she elaborated the concept of a domestic or family mode of production as a separate system from the capitalist mode of production. She has also worked on other aspects of family relations, including patterns of inheritance and the status of children within families (see Chapter 3). She has consistently insisted on the social nature of family relationships, arguing against the idea that relations between husbands and wives or parents and children are natural, and has particularly emphasized the hierarchies of gender and generation around which domestic life is ordered. Her analysis of the exploitation of women's unpaid labour within families was her major early contribution to materialist feminist theory and the foundation of her analysis of women as a class.

As we saw in the last chapter, the premise that women and men are classes is fundamental to French radical feminism. Delphy began to develop this idea from her earliest work on the domestic mode of production within which men as the exploiting class appropriated the labour of women. Other materialist feminist analyses suggest a broader foundation for class relations between women and men. Guillaumin (1981a) argues that men appropriate women both individually and collectively; a woman not appropriated by an individual man is available for appropriation by any other. This is manifested in a range of practices from sexual assault to the expectation that women, in a paid or unpaid capacity, will take on the work of caring for others. Wittig (1992), drawing on both Delphy and Guillaumin, sees the classes 'women' and 'men' as the product of institutionalized heterosexuality. This is a rather different approach from that of other feminists who emphasize sexuality and reproduction as the basis of sex-classes (for example, Ferguson, 1989; Firestone, 1972). Insofar as Guillaumin and Wittig talk of men's appropriation of women's bodies, it is clear that they mean not only appropriation for sexual and reproductive purposes, but also the appropriation of their labour. Delphy always emphasized the exploitation of women's labour, but in her later work seems to be adopting a broader definition of class relations between women and men (see Chapter 4).

Delphy's analysis of class is fundamental to her understanding of gender. Because she is so implacably opposed to essentialist ideas about women's 'difference', she sees it as vitally important that we develop an alternative perspective on the social distinctions between women and men. French materialist feminists have always maintained that 'men' and 'women' should be seen as social rather than natural categories. Hence, for example, Nicole-Claude Mathieu (1977) argues for the development of a 'social-sex' category in social analysis as something quite distinct from 'natural' sex differences. Where other materialist feminists are suspicious of the term 'gender' because it has often been used in tandem with the notion of biological sex, Delphy is committed to the term as one which emphasizes the social origins of 'men' and 'women'. In her recent work she has made significant contributions to current theories of gender (see Chapter 5).

Finally, all Delphy's work is part of a wider *political* project: the point of understanding the exploitation of women's labour, the class differences between women and men and the social construction of gender is so that we can change these social relations. She has always argued that feminist knowledge should be of use to the feminist movement. The implications of this view will be discussed in the final chapter.

Notes

1. Interview with Delphy, August 1993.

2. For an English translation of extracts from Leclerc's book, see Duchen (1987). For a more sympathetic summary of Leclerc's arguments, see Sellers (1991).

3. Another major contribution to theories of women's difference was also published in 1974, Luce Irigaray's *Speculum*. This was later subjected to a materialist feminist critique by Monique Plaza (1978). For a more general materialist feminist discussion of the concept of difference see Guillaumin's 'The question of difference' ([1979] 1987; 1995).

4. This argument is central to Delphy's analysis of women's domestic work and will be further explained in Chapter 3.

5. This is particularly evident in marxist feminist appropriations of psychoanalysis, for example Juliet Mitchell's *Psychoanalysis and Feminism* (1975), which Delphy critiqued in 'Patriarchy, feminism and their intellectuals' (Delphy, 1981b, 1984).

3

Patriarchal Relations in Families

Delphy is best known for her work on the family and particularly for the thesis that women as wives are an exploited class within a domestic mode of production. This is the position she first outlined in 'The main enemy' (1970, 1977a), continued to develop in a number of subsequent articles, and which reached its fullest exposition in *Familiar Exploitation* (1992), co-authored with Diana Leonard. *Familiar Exploitation* incorporates and elaborates upon the basic premises of Delphy's earlier writings and remains consistent with them. Since this is a coherent body of work, I will discuss it as a whole, rather than dealing separately with each of the articles which contributed to its development. In this chapter I will concentrate on the conditions of women's work within families, leaving the issue of women as a class to the next. First it is necessary to consider the political context of Delphy's early writings in order to explain the controversy that surrounded them.

In the early years of second wave feminism, housework was a central political and theoretical concern and frequently figured in attempts to explain women's subordination. Feminist writings on this issue began from certain shared assumptions: that most women, for much of their adult lives, could expect to be responsible for running a home and caring for its inhabitants, and that the work which this involved was generally undervalued, trivialized or ignored. Feminists sought to establish that housework could legitimately be defined as work and as a serious object of study, but also recognized that it differs from other work in capitalist industrial societies. Housework is unpaid and is undertaken as a personal service to others, hence it does not involve the exchange of a set number of hours or an agreed amount of work for a given return: it has no fixed job description and no clear limits. According to Delphy, the peculiarities of housework arise from the social relations within which it is performed. She has consistently argued that these relations are patriarchal and that within families men systematically exploit and benefit from women's domestic labour.[1]

This analysis provoked some very hostile responses, particularly from marxist feminists. The latter were often wary of using the concept of patriarchy because they saw capitalism as the sole or main cause of women's oppression. They were also reluctant to accept that women are exploited, the term 'exploitation' being reserved for capital's appropriation of workers' labour. Yet, as Delphy and Leonard later pointed out, this is not the only form of exploitation – under slavery, workers have all their labour directly appropriated. Marxists have been unwilling to extend this logic to the case of wives because they view capitalism as the only system that matters within modern society (Delphy and Leonard, 1992). Marxists have therefore theorized housework in terms of the contribution it made to capitalism, within what became known as 'the domestic labour debate'.[2] In the 1970s this debate dominated theoretical discussions on housework in many Western countries, particularly in Britain and Canada. It is worth looking briefly at what was at issue here since it helps to elucidate the differences between marxist and materialist feminism.[3]

The domestic labour debate

The domestic labour debate began from feminists' attempts to challenge the orthodox marxist view that housework was marginal to capitalism, but subsequently became a highly technical discussion about Marx's theory of value. The point of departure was Marx's observation that workers' wages were converted into fresh labour power and also provided for their children: the workers of the future (see Marx, 1976: 275, 717–18). Marx himself ignored the domestic work this entailed – the cooking of meals and washing of shirts necessary to make the worker ready for each new day – and the fact that this work was done largely by women. Marxist feminists initially sought to establish that this work was socially necessary, essential to the functioning of capitalism (see, for example, Benston, 1969).

Those associated with the Wages for Housework campaign argued that housework was productive labour and a hidden source of profit for capitalism (Dalla Costa and James, 1972). In marxist terms, productive labour is that which produces 'surplus value'. Put simply, part of the wealth (value) produced by workers covers their wages; the remainder, surplus value, is appropriated by capital and is the source of profit. If housewives produce labour-power and labour-power is the source of surplus value, then housework could be seen as indirectly producing surplus value. The majority of marxists, however, disagreed with this interpretation. They wished to confine the term 'productive labour' to work which directly produced surplus value, thus excluding housework. A further, and related, point of contention was whether housework itself could be said to have value or create value. Marxists generally see domestic labour as socially useful, but as having no 'exchange-value' – it is not exchanged for a wage. Similarly the products of housework, viewed by marxists as 'use-values', have no exchange value because they are not exchanged for cash. However, labour-power is seen as a commodity with an exchange value – the wage paid for it. So does a housewife produce a commodity after all: her husband's labour-power? If that commodity has an exchange-value (the man's wage), does the wife's labour-power have a hidden exchange-value incorporated into her husband's wage?

Marxists were soon tied in knots trying to answer these questions (see, for example, Coulson et al., 1975; Gardiner et al., 1975; Molyneux, 1979; Smith, 1978). The problems proved insoluble because domestic labour is not like wage labour: it is not directly exchanged for set remuneration and does not involve a fixed quantity of labour-power. It cannot, therefore, be explained in terms of a theory designed to analyse wage labour. The heat this arcane debate generated can only be understood, as Delphy and Leonard say, by the politics underlying it (see Chapter 4). It was motivated by a desire to see (working class) women as part of the proletariat, but not on the same terms as male workers. Participants in the domestic labour debate took divisions of labour between men and women for granted: they never paused to consider why it was women who performed domestic labour or why men apparently 'needed' to have it done for them. The competing claims made about the value of domestic labour were entirely contingent upon the position of the housewife's *husband* within the capitalist economy. It was in terms of *his* labour that *her* work was conceptualized. Yet relations between husbands and wives, particularly inequalities between them, were largely ignored. For most marxists, it was unthinkable that working class men might be oppressors in their own homes or that 'bourgeois' women might also be oppressed (Delphy and Leonard, 1992).

By the end of the 1970s disillusionment – and sheer boredom – with the debate was widespread. A covert consensus seems to have been arrived at whereby housework continued to be regarded as reproducing labour power but to suggest that it produced anything became almost taboo. Housework is thus talked of as reproducing, but not producing, labour-power or as 'reproduction' in some general, unspecified sense. There is a danger here of conflating the reproduction of the labour force with biological reproduction (Edholm et al., 1977; Delphy, 1980b). When women's work is said to 'reproduce' the proletariat by servicing existing workers and rearing the next generation, the implication is that they do this work because they have babies. Hence, as Delphy and Leonard say, all the complex ways in which capitalism reproduces the class system, as well as women's subordination itself, is reduced to women's reproductive capacities (1992: 59–60).

Domestic production, patriarchal exploitation

Where marxists approached housework from the perspective of the capitalist economy, Delphy looked at it from quite a different angle. Because of her research on exchange and inheritance in peasant families, she was accustomed to viewing the family as an economic system in its own right. This also, she says, enabled her to 'demystify the market' and avoid getting tangled in the distinction between use-value and exchange-value, an opposition which 'only makes sense if one takes the viewpoint of the market'. Instead of treating the non-market value of housework as a problem, she saw it as 'one of the clues to elucidating its specific nature' (1984: 16). For Delphy, housework is not excluded from the market because it is unpaid. On the contrary, it is unpaid precisely because it is excluded from the market, because it takes place within distinct, non-market social relations. These social relations are those of the *domestic mode of production* within which women's work is appropriated not by capital, but by men – more specifically, by male heads of households.[4] From this perspective, women's subordination within families is no longer seen as a side-effect of capitalism.[5]

The term 'mode of production' comes from Marx, but the idea of a specifically domestic mode of production is Delphy's own. Each mode of production involves particular forces of production – the physical means of getting productive work done – and, more importantly, particular relations of production – the social relationships entered into in the process of production. Exploitation occurs where one class of people appropriates the labour of others and/or the wealth they produce. Within the capitalist mode of production, exploitation operates through the extraction of surplus value from wage labour. Within the domestic mode of production, men as heads of households appropriate the unpaid labour of their dependants – wives and sometimes other family members. This patriarchal exploitation is perhaps more readily apparent where households produce for exchange, for example on farms or in small family enterprises. Where a man controls the means of production, the land or the business, and where the income derived from the work of all household members accrues to him, he is clearly profiting from expropriating the labour of others. Delphy argues that, even when a family relies on wages, men still appropriate their wives' labour.

This means that families must be seen as productive units. This in itself is a contentious point, challenging not only marxist thinking, but ideas which were once current in mainstream sociology. It has often been claimed that families have lost their productive function, that with industrialization 'the family changed from being a unit of production to being a unit of consumption' (Berger and Berger, 1983: 92). Such assertions rest on a very narrow definition of production – creating goods for exchange on the market – whereas Delphy has always taken a broader view of production as anything which increases wealth and produces socially useful goods and services (see Delphy and Leonard, 1992: 83). In this sense, capitalism has not removed all production from families. Delphy does not accept that housework is concerned with consumption rather than production. She challenges the conventional marxist view that housework is unpaid because it is not productive, or because it produces goods and services for use rather than exchange.

Delphy uses the example of family farms as a test case which reveals the spurious grounds on which women's domestic work is labelled unproductive. Here women's work is unpaid not only when it produces goods and services for consumption within the home, but also when it involves production for the market – as is also the case in many other small family businesses. In rural France women are often major producers of saleable goods such as milk or eggs, but they still undertake this work for their husbands (or brothers or fathers) without pay. In such households the distinction between use-value and exchange-value breaks down because much of what is produced and consumed within the family could also be exchanged on the market. The eggs with which a farmer's wife makes an omelette, for instance, could equally well have been sold for cash. Similarly, self-consumption on small farms serves to illustrate that 'there is no essential difference between activities said to be "productive" . . . and domestic activities which are called "non-productive"' (Delphy, [1977a] 1984: 64). Delphy points out that the ultimate goal of all production is consumption, that there is a continuum between production and consumption. Take the case of the farmer's wife and her eggs: the work she does rearing hens, collecting their eggs and cooking the omelette are all equally important, all involve the transformation of raw materials into something edible. It would seem absurd to view some of these tasks as productive while others are not. Yet this is what commonly happens when housework is defined as unproductive. The work the farmer's wife does up to and including egg collection would be counted as productive, but as soon as she cracks the eggs and gets out her omelette pan she is engaged in non-productive labour! The situation of farm families reveals the arbitrariness of distinctions between productive and unproductive work. Such distinctions are made by conventional economists as well as marxists – for example, when calculating a country's Gross National Product.

In much the same way, sociologists studying family enterprises have often tried to separate the 'occupational work' of wives from 'housework' – even though the women engaged in such work generally see tasks involved as interconnected (Delphy, 1978). For both sociologists and economists, the only distinguishing feature of tasks not included in occupational work, or not accounted as productive, are those tasks which are also carried out by wives in families without a business. Housework is implicitly defined as 'what is common to all households' production for consumption; and it is nowadays nearly always done by a particular female member of the family' (Delphy and Leonard, 1992: 93). 'Occupational' and 'productive' work within families thus becomes a residual category – 'what is left once "housework" is subtracted' (Delphy, [1978] 1984: 87). In other words, it is work which doesn't fall within the remit of most wives. Because most wives cook their husbands' meals, cooking is housework; because relatively few wives milk their husbands' cows, milking is not housework but occupational and productive work. What we have here is an ad hoc distinction based on a taken for granted assumption that women will normally take on a certain package of tasks without pay. Economists and sociologists take the *generality* of this unpaidness – the fact that this is unpaid work which most women do – as the basis of their distinctions between housework and other work. This does at least have the virtue of recognizing that there is something special about the work done by most women in the home because it is unpaid, but it does not explain *why* it is unpaid.

The fact that housework is unpaid cannot, then, be explained by calling it 'unproductive'. Nor is it unpaid because of the nature of the tasks performed, because every service wives provide can be bought on the market – and such services commonly are purchased when no wife is available to perform them. Conversely, women can and do earn money providing such services to those outside their families, for cleaning someone else's house, or serving meals in a restaurant: 'the same women who cooks a chop unpaid in her home is paid when she does it in another household' (Delphy, [1978] 1984: 88). So housework is not unpaid simply because it is women who do it. Rather, it is unpaid as a result of the specific social relations within which it is performed.

Delphy does not conceptualize all work done within the home as unpaid, only that done for others and appropriated by them (Delphy, 1978). She argues that doing something for oneself is not, strictly speaking, unpaid since the person doing the work benefits directly from it and is thus remunerated. For example, if I cook a meal for myself I benefit from my own work in eating the food I have prepared and in addition save myself the cost of a takeaway or restaurant – I receive some remuneration. If I cook for my partner he benefits from work he has neither done himself nor paid for – he appropriates the labour I have put into cooking his meal. 'Unpaid work' is work which not only receives no payment, but is also done for someone else and receives no remuneration because someone else appropriates it.

On the basis of these arguments, Delphy questions empirical, descriptive definitions of housework as simply what women do around the house. Instead she advances a more conceptual definition of domestic work or family work as unpaid work performed within particular, familial relations of production (Delphy, 1978). This includes what is commonly called housework, but can include other forms of work. Building upon this, Delphy and Leonard (1992) construct a three-fold distinction between housework, household work and family work. *Housework* is 'the composite of regular, day-to-day tasks which are judged necessary to maintain a home in contemporary western society' (1992: 99). Housework is not necessarily unremunerated since it might, for example, be done by a single person for him or herself or be performed for pay in someone else's home. *Household work* is 'all the work done within family household units. This includes, but is certainly not restricted to, housework alone' (1992: 100). Any work done within the household by any of its members, whether or not it is remunerated, falls into this category. It would include the work involved in running a family business and also such activities as a man doing his own car-maintenance. *Family work* is 'all the unpaid work done by dependants', within relations of dependency, and to which 'people are recruited . . . by kinship and marital relationships' (1992: 100).[6] It is this work which is appropriated by heads of household, which is subject to patriarchal exploitation within the domestic mode of production.

Delphy has always recognized that women also work outside these domestic relations, within the market economy, but the conditions under which they enter waged work serve to underline further the terms of the marital labour contract (Delphy, 1976b, 1977a). While paid employment may seem to free a woman from the total appropriation of her labour-power by her husband, she is still expected to fulfil her 'domestic responsibilities' and will usually enter employment only if she can combine both paid work and unpaid domestic work. In France a husband could legally prevent his wife from working outside the home until 1965. Wives generally seek their husbands' approval and may talk in terms of being 'allowed' to work (see, for example, Yeandle, 1984). Delphy suggests that, when a woman is employed, the costs of childcare and so on will be paid from her income, since it is assumed that she alone is responsible for this work and would normally provide it free of charge (1977a).[7] Above all, when a wife is employed the unpaid, non-exchangeable nature of domestic work is clearly revealed:

> it can no longer be claimed that she performs domestic labour in exchange for her keep, that this upkeep is the equivalent of a wage, and that therefore her work is paid, since women who go out to work keep themselves. It is therefore clear that they perform domestic work *for nothing*. (Delphy, [1977a] 1984: 68; emphasis in original)

This situation clarifies the difference between wage labour in the capitalist mode of production and work within the domestic mode. Within the former a worker sells his or her labour-power for a fixed wage, and there is an established standard of equivalence between the work done and the remuneration received. There is no such equivalence within the domestic mode of production. In return for their work wives are maintained, but this is by no means the same as receiving a wage. The services a wife provides are not fixed, they are determined by the needs and desires of her husband. The benefits she receives – the standard of living at which she is maintained – depends not on the work she does, but on the wealth and goodwill of her husband. Hence two women doing similar work may have very different standards of living. Conversely, two women may be maintained at roughly similar levels for doing different work. An example given by Delphy (1977a) is that a wife of a bourgeois man may be expected to run a large house single-handedly or she may be provided with servants to free her for the work of display. The independence of the work she does and the benefits received stems from the non-value of her work – the fact that it is not exchanged but appropriated – and because it is performed within an exclusive, personal relationship: a wife cannot change her husband as easily as a worker can change employer:

> In sum, while the wage-labourer depends on the market (on a theoretically unlimited number of employers), the married woman depends on one individual. While the wage-labourer sells his labour power, the married woman gives hers away. Exclusivity and non-payment are intimately connected. ([1977a] 1984: 71)

Because there is no fixed exchange and because women's family work constitutes a personal service for a specific individual, wives can be called upon to do a very wide range of tasks. Hence there is considerable variability in the work women actually do. In *Familiar Exploitation*, Delphy and Leonard elaborate upon the ways in which wives' work is affected by the differing circumstances and preferences of the men to whom they are married. Here they draw upon Janet Finch's pioneering study of women's incorporation into their husbands' occupations (Finch, 1983), a study which was itself influenced by Delphy's ideas. Finch does not look at all aspects of wives' domestic labour, but only that related to their husbands' work. Delphy and Leonard extend Finch's insights to consider how a husband's occupation, financial circumstances, leisure interests and personal preferences influence the precise content of the work women do.

Women's direct contributions to their husbands' work are most obvious among the self-employed, where women often work unpaid – or only nominally paid – in a man's business. In some forms of employment there is a recognized consort role for wives, as in the diplomatic service, among politicians and so on, or wives may be expected to take on specific duties such as the welfare role taken on by the wives of army officers. Even where women do not directly work for their husband's occupation, they often make part-time contributions: for example the vicar's wife offering spiritual comfort to parishioners, the academic's wife doing his proofreading and indexing. Most commonly wives provide back-up services – taking messages, filtering phone-calls and callers. This is not only required by professional men, but also active trades unionists and many small tradesmen who work from home. In addition, wives do the routine housework which frees a man to concentrate his time and energy elsewhere. In much the same way they contribute to their husbands' leisure. In addition, wives provide copious moral support through their emotional labour and also sexual services, which are often seen as a necessary part of helping a man unwind, relax and feel good.[8] Such activities are rarely reciprocal – a professional woman's husband is not expected to act as a visible consort, entertain her colleagues or provide secretarial back-up – let alone devote himself to creating home comforts for her.

A husband's work and leisure structures his wife's life in a variety of ways. Where they live, the internal organization of domestic space, her time and her domestic routine are dictated by his work and leisure. Wives do not have a discrete workload which, once completed, leaves them free to do other things. Their marital obligation is to devote whatever time and energy is necessary to do what their husbands require of them. This might include wage labour if household income is low, or leaving it if it conflicts with other responsibilities. A point which is constantly reiterated throughout Delphy's work is that wives do not own their labour-power because their husbands always have a claim on it. They are not free to sell their labour-power on the same terms as men: one cannot freely sell what one does not fully own.

Within families women's labour is effectively owed to and controlled by their husbands or household head. Delphy and Leonard call attention to the hierarchies of gender and age evident in family production (1986, 1992). Recent French studies of farm families, some of which, like Finch's work, are influenced by Delphy's theoretical position, yield much supporting evidence for their claims. Farming in France is still a family activity, although the effective unit of production is usually a couple – young people are now unwilling to work unpaid on the farm. Men usually restrict themselves to agricultural work, while wives do both farm work and housework. Although women often have their own specific agricultural responsibilities – such as feeding animals or making cheese – they can be asked to do almost anything. They are on hand whenever their husband needs their help as farm labourers and are expected to drop what they are doing to assist him. They thus have little autonomy even in carrying out their own designated household chores. Moreover, the tasks done by family members carry varying amounts of prestige and generally adult men do the high status work. Often this is explained by the functional necessity of tasks or by the capacities of individuals – such as physical strength – but what counts as high status or 'heavy' work is highly variable and can hardly be judged as such by objective criteria. Driving a tractor is men's work, hefting large bales of hay on to the tractor trailer is women's work. What makes particular work 'women's work' is not the allocation of specific chores to them, but that 'the status, the conditions of doing it, the relations of production of the work, are specific to family subordinates' (Delphy and Leonard, 1992: 135). These status differentials are not restricted to farm families, but are generally observable in divisions of household work elsewhere.

All this implies a power structure within which the household head manages labour and takes decisions. Delphy and Leonard suggest that his control is often not recognized because who does what depends on custom, or because delegated control – such as the wife's responsibility for the kitchen – is misread as total control. Wives doing unpaid family work have to be granted some autonomy in order to be able to carry out their responsibilities effectively, but again this is delegated autonomy. Subordinates may influence the decisions taken by the head, may make him change his mind, 'but the mind to be changed is his' (Delphy and Leonard, 1992: 137). Although in principle many men and women support an egalitarian ideal, in practice the power relationship between them persists and is taken for granted. Delphy and Leonard are not saying that husbands' power is never challenged, but that its existence is evident in the control men exercise over the family economy. This is not a matter of individual men's sexism, but is built into the family system.

Delphy and Leonard argue that subordinates who earn their own income may find their bargaining power increased, but that their money is not fully theirs. It is usually allowed for by the head, who implicitly determines what it is to be used for, for example by reducing his contribution to housekeeping or by earmarking it for his wife's 'personal spending' so that he does not have to buy her clothes. Hence 'wives do not have the same rights to control the money they earn as their husbands or boyfriends have to the money they earn' (Delphy and Leonard, 1992: 118). Here it begins to become clear that inequalities in consumption are related to the exploitative structure of family production.

Sociologists who speak of families as 'units of consumption' tend to ignore the unequal distribution of resources within them and, indeed, have often assumed that domestic consumption is organized on an equitable basis. Similarly government statistics and market researchers tend to treat families as undifferentiated units of consumption. In a pioneering article Delphy challenged this view (Delphy, 1979). Not all consumption by family members takes place within families and even that which does cannot be assumed to be communal and egalitarian: rather, it is ordered by hierarchies of gender and generation. Delphy backs her theoretical argument, once again, with evidence from rural France, where a man's position as head of both family and farm entitles him to the best of whatever is available. Resources within families are distributed according to the same principles which govern the division of labour – according to the status of those receiving them. What men consume carries prestige, what carries prestige is consumed by men. It is not, as has generally been assumed by sociologists and lay people, that consumption within families is determined by individual needs. Moreover, need itself is socially defined, so that even when women engage in heavy agricultural work they are not deemed to 'need' meat or wine to give them strength while men are assumed to have such 'needs'. In poor families even food is not equitably distributed, while among the more affluent differential consumption becomes evident in a wider variety of arenas (Delphy, 1979; Delphy and Leonard, 1992).[9]

As Delphy (1979) points out, domestic purchases may be collective, but actual consumption is necessarily individual. Even where a family appears to be consuming things simultaneously and collectively, its members are not necessarily consuming exactly the same items in exactly the same way. An example of this, revealed by recent studies of media consumption, is the case of family television viewing. Even when a family watches the same programme together, there are likely to be differences in how it is being watched. The choice of programme is frequently dictated by the head of household who typically gives it his full attention. His wife will often be engaged in some chore, such as ironing or mending, while she watches television and may be in and out of the room fetching him beer or tea or supervising the children. The children, meanwhile, may be half watching the programme while engaging in other pursuits (Moores, 1993; Morley, 1986). The television set, then, may be seen as a collective possession of the family as a whole, but is not consumed equally by all.

Thus domestic consumption is both quantitatively and qualitatively differentiated. This is related to exploitation in families, because those who are exploited are maintained rather than paid. Hence, Delphy argues, much of their consumption is not free consumption: having a coat bought for you, for example, is not the same as buying one for yourself. Furthermore, women's work in the home is intimately tied to immediate consumption, thus they frequently cannot consume in the same way as others. A woman who cooks and serves a meal does not consume it in the same way as those she cooks for and waits upon. Moreover, what is consumed in the home involves not just commodities, but the labour entailed in preparing them for consumption. This is a highly personalized service – having meals prepared how and when you want them, the precise clothes you need washed and ironed and ready for appropriate occasions. Wives do this for others; they rarely have such services provided for them. These inequalities of consumption are so commonplace that women's self-sacrifice goes unnoticed – imposing restrictions on oneself and leaving the best for others is an accepted part of being a good wife and mother (Delphy, 1979, 1984; Delphy and Leonard, 1992).

The congruence between patterns of work and patterns of consumption within families are not merely coincidental, but is integral to the patriarchal structure of families within which men exploit the labour of their wives and control economic resources. Because of this women do not have the right to consume on equal terms with their husbands – they do not, as is sometimes assumed, share equally in a common marital fund. As we have seen, it is false to assume that a wife is not really unpaid because her husband maintains her. Not only does this maintenance have no direct relation to the work she does, but is additionally determined by her husband's income and his control over consumption. A husband may have an obligation to maintain a wife, just as she has an obligation to work for him, but these are distinct obligations: each exists independently of how adequately the other is fulfilled. However mean a man is, his wife is still expected to do domestic work and, conversely, however bad a housewife she is, he is still expected to maintain her. The non-exchange typical of the domestic mode of production is evident both in production and consumption.

There is one further aspect of economic relations within families that should be mentioned here: the question of inheritance or the transmission of property within and between generations. Sociologists have generally thought of inheritance in terms of differences between families, as a means by which wealthy families preserve their privileges vis à vis poorer families. From her earliest work on transmission within French farm families, Delphy has always been aware that inheritance also serves to preserve inequalities within families (Delphy, 1969). The transmission of property and rank are gendered: while women can and do own and inherit property, the patriarchal bias in our inheritance system usually means that they inherit less. In rural farming families as well as among more prosperous property owners this has served to keep productive resources in the hands of men. People's occupations are now more often mediated by the education system than by inheritance, but it is not unusual for more to be invested in a son's education than a daughter's. Many, of course, lack property or advantages to pass on to their children. Here it is the gendered labour market rather than patrimonial transmission that deprives women of access to adequate means of subsistence and pushes them into domestic relations of production (Delphy and Leonard, 1992).

This brings us to the relationship between women's unpaid work within families and their low paid work in the market economy. Although Delphy suggests that wives enter employment only if it fits in with their husbands' demands on their time, she also points to a causal link operating in the opposite direction; because women have been marginalized in the labour market, with adverse effects on their capacity to earn, marriage may offer them a better chance of economic security than remaining single:

> the situation created for women in the labour market itself constitutes an objective incentive to marry, and hence . . . the labour market plays a role in the exploitation of their domestic labour. (Delphy, 1984: 20)

Marriage is also in this respect 'a self-perpetuating state' (Delphy, 1976b: 80), since women's earning capacity relative to that of their husbands tends to decline over time. If women take breaks from paid work to fulfil family obligations, this further disadvantages them in the labour market. If they continue to be employed, they may have to restrict their hours of work or their place of work to fit in with their husband's requirements. They will certainly not be able to give the single-minded attention to their work that married men can. Men are freed to concentrate on paid work because their wives do domestic work for them, while married women still do domestic work in addition to paid work. Hence ' ten years after the wedding day marriage is even more necessary than before' (1976b: 80).[10] For a woman 'marriage creates the conditions for its own continuation and encourages entry into a second marriage if a particular union comes to an end' (1976b: 81). There is thus a complex interrelationship between women's paid and unpaid work.

It should be clear from this that Delphy does not consider the domestic mode of production to be the sole institutional basis of patriarchy. As we have seen in the previous chapter, she is suspicious of monocausal explanations of women's subordination. Nor does she argue that women's exploitation within households determines other forms of sexual inequality, nor even that her analysis covers all aspects of family life. This is sometimes misunderstood. In the concluding section of 'The main enemy', she asserts that patriarchal exploitation is the common, specific and main oppression of women. It is common because it affects all married women, specific because only women are under obligation to provide free domestic services, and main because the expectation that women will marry and become housewives conditions their participation in other spheres of life. She qualifies this statement, however, by drawing attention to gaps in her analysis, in particular that she has not considered how the exploitation of women's reproductive capacities related to exploitation of their productive capacities, nor how patriarchal exploitation interconnects with capitalist exploitation (Delphy, 1977a: 28–9) In her later work she is still more careful to define the limits of her own enquiries. Even in *Familiar Exploitation*, which covers aspects of domestic relationships, such as sexual and emotional labour, which Delphy had not considered elsewhere, it is explicitly stated that this work does not constitute an exhaustive analysis of the family.

Objections to Delphy's analysis of patriarchal exploitation

After the publication in pamphlet form of *The Main Enemy* in 1977, Delphy's work came under heavy fire from marxist feminists. She herself has countered many of their objections in an early response to criticism (Delphy, 1980b), and has subsequently dealt with more in further clarifications of her position. She has also been defended by others, such as Janet Finch (1983) and Sylvia Walby (1986a, 1990), both of whom have found her theories productive. Those outside marxist circles, particularly feminists based in the United States, have often not understood what was at stake in these debates and hence Delphy's distance from marxist feminism. As we have seen in the last chapter, some now identifying themselves as 'materialist feminists' classify Delphy's work as part of the same tradition as that of her marxist feminist critics. Similarly the prominent radical feminist, Catherine MacKinnon, locates Delphy within what she calls '"wages for housework" theory' (1989: 64), apparently unaware of the differences between Delphy's position and that of Dalla Costa or other participants in the domestic labour debate.

One common criticism of Delphy is easy to deal with – that her work on the domestic mode of production does not explain other aspects of women's subordination. Barrett and McIntosh (1979), Beechey (1979) and Barrett (1980) all treat her work as if it amounts to an all-encompassing theory of women's subordination. Sometimes the result is gross misrepresentation. According to Beechey, for example, Delphy thinks that 'the family has primacy over all other social relationships' and assumes 'that patriarchy resides only in the family' (Beechey, 1979: 71). Generally Delphy is admonished for not specifying the links between the domestic mode of production and the capitalist mode and for focusing exclusively on the family. Barrett and McIntosh also berate her for concentrating on the material aspects of domestic life. As Delphy herself says in her defence, it was never her intention to explain everything (1980b: 92), hence she is being criticized for failing to do what she never set out to do in the first place. In part such misunderstandings arose from the political context of the time. Marxist feminists were used to seeing marxism as a body of theory which could explain everything and hence evaluated alternatives in these terms. Moreover, feminists of many different persuasions were at that time engaged in a search for the root cause of women's oppression and this may have affected the way Delphy's work was interpreted, although she herself was always wary of such totalizing explanations (Delphy, 1984).

Most criticisms of her amount to the accusation that she is insufficiently marxist. Because she refuses to accord capitalism primacy in determining *all* social relations, she is accused of hostility to marxism (Barrett and McIntosh, 1979; Molyneux, 1979), and because she applies marxist concepts and methods to the analysis of patriarchy rather than capitalism, she is held to misuse those concepts and methods (Barrett and McIntosh, 1979; Kaluzynska, 1980; Molyneux, 1979). As Delphy (1980b) points out, she can hardly be seen as hostile to marxism when she employs its methods. What she is opposed to is 'a religious attitude to the writings of Marx' (1980b: 83), which treats his works as incontrovertible truth, and to those, like Barrett and McIntosh (1979), who claim to speak from a position of divine authority by virtue of their marxism:

> [They] then come to judge real oppression, and even the very existence of oppression, according to whether or not it corresponds to 'Marxism', and not Marxism according to whether or not it is pertinent to real oppressions. (Delphy, 1980b: 84)

Most of these keepers of the faith focus on Delphy's deviations from established marxist dogma rather than the utility of her arguments for understanding women's subordinate position within families. Central to these charges of heresy is Delphy's claim that there are two modes of production coexisting in our society (Barrett and McIntosh, 1979; Kaluzynska, 1980; Molyneux, 1979). Kaluzynska, for example, asserts that Delphy's use of the term 'mode of production':

> transfers terms borrowed from historical periodization to describe subjective impressions of oppression . . . The term is part of the technical vocabulary of Marxism. It is not a mere synonym for 'the way housewives do things'. (Kaluzynska, 1980: 40–1)

This scathing dismissal of Delphy's work as mere description is not unique; Barrett and McIntosh (1979) make a similar point, as does Molyneux (1979). It is difficult, however, to see how anyone could so misread Delphy: she is clearly dealing analytically with the social relations within which women's domestic labour is exploited, not simply describing 'the way housewives do things', as Kaluzynska puts it, or a 'way of producing' (Molyneux, 1979: 16). It was not simply the idea of a separate domestic mode of production which provoked such ire. Harrison's (1973) conceptualization of a 'housework mode of production', while contested, was treated as a serious contribution to marxist theory (see, for example, Gardiner et al., 1975; Kuhn and Wolpe, 1978: 199). Unlike Delphy, Harrison argues that the housework mode of production exists to service capitalism and that the surplus labour extracted from housewives passes not to their husbands but, via their husbands' wage labour, to capital. Delphy posed more of a challenge to traditional marxism in asserting that men, rather than capital, exploit and benefit from women's domestic labour. Molyneux is critical of both perspectives, although she reserves her more caustic comments for Delphy.

Both Molyneux and Kaluzynska see modes of production primarily as historical epochs and argue that two modes of production cannot exist side by side unless a society is in transition between them. There is, however, no consensus among marxists on this matter (see Walby, 1986a). One mode of production identified by Marx – slavery – has historically always operated in association with some other mode. There are no a priori grounds on which marxism excludes the possibility of there being more than one mode of production within one society. Even some of those who question the existence of a patriarchal mode of production, such as Barrett and McIntosh (1979), concede this point. However, they still wish to preserve the concept of mode of production as a means of characterizing the entire social formation:

> the usefulness of the concept of mode of production . . . lies in the fact that it enables us to identify the material base of the social formation in each historical epoch . . . the historical development of a society can be understood in relation to the replacement of one mode of production by another. (Barrett and McIntosh, 1979: 99)

Thus it is decided in advance that our society can only be described as capitalist, that patriarchal relations are of secondary importance, and that therefore there can be no patriarchal mode of production.

Barrett and McIntosh, like most marxists, accept that 'domestic work involves very different relations of production from wage work', but assert that this is 'insufficient basis for claiming that there is a distinct mode of production here' (1979: 98). Given that a mode of production is a specific combination of forces and relations of production, then logically all that disqualifies domestic production from being a distinct mode of production is the lack of separate forces or means of production. This would seem to give undue weight to the forces of production which are not usually conceptualized as having an existence independent of the relations of production within which they operate. Walby (1986a) suggests that the relations of domestic production limit the development of forces of production because economies of scale and socialized labour are ruled out. Particular domestic technologies may have been developed as a result of industrial capitalism, but the ways in which these technologies are deployed in domestic production are quite different from the ways in which they are used in capitalist production. Walby also argues that the head of household, because of his control over economic resources, effectively owns the domestic means of production and may decide what equipment is bought.

Molyneux takes the view that there are no means of domestic production at all:

> What are the means of production in a mode in which there is no social production and the product is in the form of some of the housewife's surplus labour? It is doubtful whether the creation of use values for private consumption, whether by cooking or gardening, justifies the use of the concept 'means of production' to designate implements utilized in such activities. (Molyneux, 1979: 18)

Molyneux denies the possibility of there being any 'means of production' involved in the domestic sphere simply because she has already decided that there is no production going on here. Domestic labour is deemed by definitional fiat to produce nothing and to have no means of producing anything. It becomes instead an act of 'creation'. This is an example of the sort of mystificatory use of marxist concepts of which Delphy is so critical . The 'product' of the domestic mode of production in Delphy's analysis is not 'the housewife's surplus labour', but the goods and services she produces. In Molyneux's formulation 'use-values' becomes an abstraction through which these material products are disguised. We are told that no 'social production' is involved because marxists reserve the term 'social production' for production for exchange; this has the effect of denying that what goes on within families is 'social' and hence risks the imputation that it must, therefore, be 'natural' (see Delphy and Leonard, 1986).

Delphy's work is also criticized for its lack of attention to history and failure to address the relationship between the capitalist and patriarchal modes of production (Barrett, 1980, 1988; Barrett and McIntosh, 1979; Beechey, 1979; Molyneux, 1979). It is true that

Delphy concentrates on patriarchy alone. She feels that until we have understood patriarchy we will be unable to determine how it interconnects with capitalism (Delphy, 1977a: 19). It is therefore a misrepresentation of Delphy to claim, as Molyneux and Barrett and McIntosh do, that she sees patriarchal mode of production as totally autonomous from other modes. Delphy often refers in passing to historical changes, but her primary focus is on patriarchy here and now – how it operates in modern Western society. This does not mean that it is an ahistorical concept – on the contrary she is very resistant to transhistorical conceptualizations of patriarchy (Delphy, 1984: 17–18). Molyneux makes a further criticism on this theme: that Delphy does not adequately confront 'the question of the historical and cultural specificity of housework' (1979: 15). Molyneux argues, correctly, that while some aspects of housework pre-date capitalism its precise content has changed. This insight is hardly antithetical to Delphy's analysis, since she devotes considerable attention to challenging definitions of domestic labour as simply a series of chores. Given that she emphasizes that the work women do within families depends on what their husbands require of them, it follows that it is historically variable. Although Delphy herself has not analysed these changes, it is possible to develop a materialist feminist analysis of the history of housework (see Jackson, 1992a) and of the intersections between patriarchy and capitalism more generally (Walby, 1986a). Charges of ahistoricity, then, once again rest on criticizing Delphy for not doing what she never set out to do in the first place. The limits Delphy has chosen to impose on her own enquiries do not necessarily define the boundaries of her theory's utility.

Another supposed 'limitation' of Delphy's work is her use of evidence from French farming families. This is said to be insufficient to support 'the theoretical edifice which rests upon it' (Barrett and McIntosh, 1979: 100). Similarly, Delphy's analysis is held to have little general validity because of 'the specificity of her data and the empiricist derivations of her theory' (Molyneux, 1979: 7). These dismissive comments are based on a misreading of Delphy's work. As she says in her own defence, she does not base her entire 'theoretical edifice' on the situation of farm families. Rather she uses this evidence to counter the claim that housework is unpaid because it does not produce goods for exchange, and to demonstrate that it is the labour relationship of marriage, rather than the tasks women perform, which accounts for it being unpaid (see Delphy, 1980b: 92). The example of such families is used to further an analytical argument, not to establish an empirical foundation for her theory. Moreover, some aspects of economic relations within family businesses may not be as anachronistic as these critics claim and may, indeed, be of wider applicability than Delphy herself initially realized. In 'The main enemy' she states that the work of most wives is now limited to production for family consumption and that 'the number of independent workers who can exchange the labour of their wives is diminishing, while the number of wage earners who cannot exchange this labour is increasing' (1977a: 11). She thus assumes that male wage earners exchange only their own and not their wives' labour. Janet Finch questions this, arguing that 'there is a real sense in which wage labourers can and do exchange their wives' unpaid labour as their own and derive significant benefits thereby' (1983: 10). Finch suggests that there are a number of occupations where wives may make a direct contribution to their husbands' jobs. The wives of country policemen and doctors, clergymen, diplomats, army officers and academics all, officially or unofficially, do work for which their husbands are paid. These men are then exchanging their wives' labour (Finch, 1983: 99–106). As we have seen, this insight was later taken up by Delphy and Leonard (1986).

The most contentious aspect of Delphy's work is her claim that men exploit and benefit from women's domestic work. Marxist feminists find this hard to accept, and it is one of the main reasons, perhaps *the* main reason, why the existence of the domestic mode of production is denied. Delphy's critics keep reminding us of the exploitation that men face as wage labourers, as if this absolves proletarian men from any responsibility for the oppression of women. Barrett and McIntosh accuse Delphy of looking at only one half of the household and ignoring the relations of production which men enter into. Therefore, they say, she does not see that the situation of proletarian men is different from that of petit bourgeois or peasant men because the former's 'principle productive activity is in the social sphere of wage labour' and their contribution to the domestic economy is through their wage (1979: 98–9). We are presumably to infer that, even if farmers and petit bourgeois men exploit their wives, proletarians do not. The counter-argument here is best left in Delphy's own words:

> . . . it appears . . . that I have not seen what I never stop shouting from the roof-tops – i.e. that men and women have different relations of production. But obviously Barrett and McIntosh aim *not to see* these differences since their goal is to try to annul them by speaking of the 'domestic economy' as a whole indissolubly constituted of the wife's work and the man's wage . . . The fact that this mutual dependence is not exactly reciprocal and that this allows one of the indissociable elements to disassociate its interests enough from the other element to exploit it, is not something they want to see. (1980b: 92–3; emphasis in original)

Molyneux is also reluctant to admit that men and women might have different material interests. She argues that men's appropriation of women's labour, even if it can be shown to happen, is not sufficient to justify the use of the term 'exploitation' since exploitation 'has to be given at the level of the relations of production' (Molyneux, 1979: 14). Delphy does of course establish this, but in terms of domestic relations of production. 'The' relations of production referred to by Molyneux, on the other hand, are those of capitalism; once again, capitalism is the only system that matters. Later she suggests that appropriation is not exploitation because when a man works as a wage labourer, his wage funds the family's subsistence and hence 'he performs some "surplus labour" which is "appropriated" by his wife and children'. Does this, she asks 'turn *them* into *his exploiters*?' (Molyneux, 1979: 18; emphasis in original). This is indeed, as she says, an improbable conclusion. Molyneux seeks to convince us that the idea of exploitation happening in families is self-evidently ludicrous. In so doing she presupposes that the maintenance a man provides is a fair exchange for the work his wife does. As we have seen, Delphy argues that no standard of equivalence exists – let alone a fair one – and a woman is expected to supply unpaid family labour even when she earns her own subsistence. Molyneux's argument rests on an unwillingness to accept that families, particularly those of proletarians, are fundamentally inegalitarian.

This is also the case with the critique advanced by Barrett

(1980). She accepts that men may benefit generally from women's subordination, but, she says, 'it is not so clear that they benefit specifically from the present organization of the household' (1980: 216). She contends that the role of breadwinner is not an intrinsically desirable one since family responsibilities tie men to wage labour and that, while men 'evade domestic labour and responsibility for childcare', they lose out in other ways: they are deprived of 'significant access to children' and are subject to a 'rigid definition of masculinity' which is itself oppressive (1980: 217). However, a wife is not, as Barrett implies, simply a dependant whom her husband's wage must support: she works for him, enabling him to devote his attention to earning the wage which he controls (Walby, 1986a). Men do not just 'evade' housework and childcare – it is not that they do not do their share, but that they have their share done for them. That men may suffer a loss of potential personal satisfactions in no way balances the material benefits they gain from their exploitation of their wives' labour. It might just as well be argued that capitalists do not really benefit from the exploitation of wage labour since they might have more meaningful relationships with others, and feel better about themselves, if it were not for the constraints which being capitalists placed upon them! No marxist would advance such a case.

Women of course care for others as well as their husbands. This too has been used as a way of discrediting Delphy's arguments. Barrett and McIntosh ask: 'Are we to see children and the old and disabled as exploiters?'(1979: 102). This is a disingenuous question since it is self-evident that these recipients of women's care do not occupy the same position in the domestic economy as husbands. Men are cared for, or served, as heads of household; children are cared for as dependants (and subordinates). The material relationship between mother and child is in no way the same as that between wife and husband. Moreover, as Delphy reminds us, children have fathers as well as mothers, hence 'services applied *to* children are not appropriated *by* them but by the person who would have to perform (half of) the work if his wife did not provide the totality, i.e. the husband' (1980b: 93).

While dependant children cannot be said to exploit their mothers, it is possible that an adult child could exploit her – or more credibly his – mother's labour if he or she became head of household. Similarly, sick or elderly relatives may exploit their carers if they are heads of households, but not if they are dependants. The only kin able to appropriate and exploit women's labour in the same way as husbands are those, usually men, who are household heads. This clears up another misconception. According to Barrett and McIntosh (1979), Delphy's use of the term patriarchy is ambiguous because it sometimes refers to husbands' appropriation of their wives' labour and at other times the domination of the father over the whole family. For Delphy, however, 'the power of the husband and the power of the father are not opposed'(1980b: 93), since both are the power of the head of household, potentially enabling him to exploit the labour of his wife, children or any other dependant relatives.

A further objection raised by both Barrett and McIntosh (1979) and Molyneux (1979) is that not all women marry. This, however, does not invalidate the concept of the domestic mode of production; it simply means that at any given time some women are not immediately subject to the particular form of exploitation it entails. This does not mean that unmarried women are therefore unaffected by patriarchy nor that Delphy is saying, as Barrett and McIntosh would have us believe, that women can escape oppression by the simple expedient of remaining unmarried. On the contrary, Delphy insists that the exploitation of domestic work affects all women, it is fundamental to their disadvantaged position in the labour market and is evident in the stigma still attached to spinsterhood (Delphy, 1980b: 94). Women living independently of men, even as heads of household, do not have the same status as male household heads since they lack the advantage of having a wife (Delphy and Leonard, 1992).

Barrett and McIntosh argue that it is not marriage which is fundamental to women's oppression, but motherhood, and suggest that the way forward is through analysis of the latter:

> An analysis of childcare and women's position with regard to the reproduction of the species would lead to an analysis of the role of women in reproducing labour power, and the forces and relations of capitalist production generally. (Barrett and McIntosh, 1979: 102)

As Delphy says, we 'are confronted here with biologism of an amazing crudeness' which reduces social reproduction to women's capacity to bear children (Delphy, 1980b: 94). It is also, of course, another version of the old story that women's oppression can only be understood in terms of its usefulness to capitalism.

All of the criticisms of Delphy considered so far have focused on the economics of domestic labour. Some of her detractors, however, suggest that economic analysis cannot explain women's oppression. This is a minor element of Molyneux's critique, but is far more central to Barrett and McIntosh (see also Adlam, 1979). Delphy (1980b) suggests that Barrett and McIntosh's two lines of attack on her are in fact incompatible: on the one hand they argue that she gets her economic analysis wrong, and on the other claim that this sort of analysis cannot, in any case, explain women's subordination. This is in part explicable by the gradual move away from materialist analysis among marxist feminists, a move just getting under way at the time of this debate. Having decided that marxist economic concepts were inapplicable to women's oppression, many began to look to theories of ideology and to psychoanalysis for explanations.[11]

Delphy contests Barrett and McIntosh's (1979) claim that she denies the role of ideology in perpetuating women's subordination. Where Barrett and McIntosh often speak of the ideological and economic as alternative forms of analysis, Delphy insists on their interrelationship (Delphy, 1979: 100).[12] She would agree that we need to examine the ideological processes 'by which women are constituted as a category' (Barrett and McIntosh, 1979: 100), and has subsequently devoted considerable attention to this process (see Chapter 5). She insists, however, that these ideological categories are rooted in material hierarchies. Delphy argues that we need to understand material inequalities in order to be able to discern the workings of ideology, since ideology serves to conceal material conditions:

> It is easy to say now that the opinion that women who are at home all day 'do nothing' is 'ideological', but who knew it ten years ago? Without those who showed that housework was work, where would those who now talk of the 'ideology of domestic work' be? (Delphy, 1980b: 100)

Variations in Western family forms

A further objection raised by Delphy's critics is that she ignores the economic differences among families and therefore the different conditions under which women within them perform domestic labour (Barrett and McIntosh, 1979; Molyneux, 1979). More recently, the concept of 'the family' has itself been called into question, with some sociologists and feminists suggesting that it is more of an ideological construct than a lived reality, that households are too diverse to allow us to use such a monolithic term as 'the family' and that only a minority of households are 'families' (see, for example, Barrett and McIntosh, 1982).

In *Familiar Exploitation* Delphy and Leonard contest this view. They use the term 'family' to mean a domestic residential group based on a heterosexual couple and children. As they point out, the distinction between households and families 'has been used by some writers as a way of suggesting that households are only sometimes, contingently, or as a matter of choice, based upon family relations' (1992: 5). They argue that, on the contrary, the familial basis of households is part of our social system – it is not an accident. It may be the case that only a minority of households are nuclear families if this is narrowly defined, but most people in Western societies – about 80 per cent – live in households whose members are related by marriage and/or descent. Most of those who do not live in families have done so or will do so at some point in their lives: 'We see the familial basis of domestic groups as an important element in continuing the patriarchal nature of our society: that is, in the continuance of men's dominance over women and children in the West' (1992: 5). This does not imply that the family is in any sense a natural unit, since Delphy and Leonard are emphatically opposed to 'naturalistic' assumptions about the family which conceal the social nature of gender, heterosexuality, marriage and parenthood. Nor do they ignore diversity among families. As we have seen they give considerable attention to the variety of work undertaken by wives in different social contexts.

Delphy and Leonard do, however, give scant attention to ethnic variations in family forms. Black feminists have been very critical of white feminists' condemnation of the family. It has been argued that black families are sites of solidarity and resistance to racism; they are also frequently under attack from racist state agencies and policies (Bhavnani and Coulson, 1986; Carby, 1982; hooks, 1982; Parmar, 1982). It is not argued that black families are egalitarian, but rather that other sites of oppression are more important and that racism profoundly affects the experience of family life. Hence it is still possible to argue that women from all ethnic groups in the West are likely to be subject to patriarchal exploitation within households. However, their labour may be exploited in different ways, and perhaps to different degrees, because of variations in the form of economic contract between husbands and wives. These variations are not only a reflection of cultural diversity, but are also the product of imperialism and racism. Here we should take account of historical factors which have affected modern family forms – such as the history of slavery and divisions of labour within colonial empires – as well as the continuing effects of racism. The complex interplay between all these factors has produced the differences in family structures currently observable in the West.

Few Afro-Caribbean and Afro-American women have the chance to be full-time economically dependant housewives and are more likely to live in women-headed households (Carby, 1982; Coonz, 1988; hooks, 1982). They are not, however, necessarily free from the obligation to do housework for men (see Thorogood, 1987). South Asian women more commonly live in male-headed households and in extended families than women of either European or African descent. Those who are Muslim are also less likely to be engaged in wage-labour outside the home. Among South and East Asian groups there is a strong tradition of family based enterprise, which can mean women working for little or no wages within family businesses (Afshar, 1989; Baxter and Raw, 1988; Bhachu, 1988). In addition, black women from a variety of ethnic backgrounds have historically often worked as servants, freeing privileged white women from the more menial aspects of domestic labour.

Despite these differences in household structure and organization across the diverse range of ethnic groups within Western societies, it is commonly accepted that housework is women's work. Women may share work with other women in extended family households, may combine domestic work with paid work, or may engage in production for exchange within family enterprises. Delphy's concept of the domestic mode of production can potentially encompass all these variations in family structures: as long as this mode of production is not thought of as a static, inflexible entity, variations in its form are no grounds for denying its existence.

Patriarchy and capitalism: Walby's development of Delphy

Delphy has never developed an analysis of the interrelationship between the domestic and capitalist modes of production, but Sylvia Walby has done so, drawing both on Delphy's work and that of Heidi Hartmann (Walby, 1986a, 1989, 1990). Hartmann is one of the few marxist feminists to argue that patriarchy has a material base, that it rests on men's control over women's labour and that men directly benefit from this control (1981). Hartmann's perspective is in many respects congruent with Delphy's, although she does not employ the concept of the domestic mode of production. She says less than Delphy about patriarchal power within families, but devotes considerable attention to paid employment and the intersection of patriarchy with capitalism. Walby synthesizes elements of both theorists' work. However, her analysis of the patriarchal mode of production – a term she uses to emphasize its mode of exploitation – owes more to Delphy. Like Delphy, Walby does not consider the patriarchal mode of production to be the sole basis of patriarchy, but she provides an analysis of its operation, and its articulation with the capitalist mode, in terms technical enough to placate the most pedantic of Delphy's marxist critics.

Domestic labour can be said to produce two things; first, the goods and services consumed by family members, and, second, labour-power which is sold in exchange for wages. Whereas Delphy talks of exploitation primarily in terms of the first of these types of production, Walby analyses it in relation to the second. These two forms of production are of course inextricably interlinked. In the process of cooking and serving food, for example, a woman produces a meal, but she is at the same time contributing to the production of the labour-power of those who consume that meal: herself, her husband and her children. Walby defines the main object of women's labour as the exhausted labour power that she works to replenish. The husband is able to exploit his wife's labour because he has effective possession of the means of domestic production in a way that she does not. He is himself one of the objects of production; she works on him and for him to replenish the labour-power which he controls. Her body, on the other hand, is one of the instruments of production, in which he has rights by virtue of the marriage contract. Other instruments of production – tools, appliances and so on – may be jointly owned, but as the primary breadwinner with ultimate control over finances, he has the final say in deciding which instruments will be purchased.

Whereas Delphy analyses domestic production and exploitation in terms of what goes on within families, Walby concentrates on the intersection between patriarchal exploitation and the market economy of capitalism – hence her emphasis on the production of labour-power. Walby argues that a man realizes the value of the surplus labour he has appropriated from his wife when he sells his labour-power. His control over this labour-power and the wage he receives for it is central to the process of exploitation. He 'uses and exchanges that labour power with an employer as if it were his own, even though his wife laboured to produce it' (Walby, 1986a: 53). The wages which the man then receives are not shared equally. He typically spends more on himself than she spends on herself while she works longer hours for less return. This difference, according to Walby 'may be regarded as the wife's surplus labour which he has appropriated'. He is able to exert such financial power 'because he has control over the labour power she has produced and hence over the wage he received from the capitalist in exchange for it'. Therefore, she concludes 'domestic labour is exploited' (Walby, 1986a: 54). This is a rather different view of exploitation from that of Delphy. For Delphy, the amount of maintenance a woman receives is not the issue: it is the fact that she is maintained rather than paid which underpins her exploitation.

The patriarchal mode of production, like any other mode, takes varying forms and changes over time. The exploitation of women's labour within households, the defining feature of the patriarchal mode of production, well pre-dates capitalism. Walby sees the transition to capitalism as crucial to its modern form, but not in the sense of totally determining it. This history has entailed both accommodation and tension between capitalism and patriarchy, and men have defended patriarchal privileges under changing socio-economic conditions. Change has been particularly rapid over the last two decades:

> Women are no longer necessarily bound to an individual husband who expropriates their labour til death do them part. Instead, increasing numbers of women change husbands, have children without husbands and engage in work for an employer other than their husband. Women spend a smaller proportion of their life-time's labour under patriarchal relations of production. (Walby, 1990: 89)

Walby sees these changes as part of a shift from private to public patriarchy, with control of individual women in families and households giving way to public control through the state, the labour market and so on. This implies that the patriarchal mode of production is declining in importance within the social structure as a whole, a conclusion which Delphy and Leonard (1992) contest. In particular, they argue that the entry of married women into paid employment intensifies their exploitation in the home since they are no longer maintained in exchange for the unpaid labour they continue to perform. Where Walby regards married women as controlling their own labour-power when they exchange it for wages, Delphy and Leonard argue that they are not as free to sell their labour-power on the market as are men. Moreover, the fact that women leave men or change partners does not spell the end of marriage as an institution – and most women continue to marry or cohabit. As Delphy has long argued, marriage and divorce are interdependent; there are continuities as well as discontinuities between marriage and divorce (Delphy, 1976b), which becomes clear when the relationship between marriage and childcare is subjected to scrutiny.

Children in families

As we have seen, Delphy is resistant to analyses of women's subordination which reduce it to their responsibility for children, but she does see this as one aspect of patriarchal exploitation. She suggests that a husband appropriates his wife's labour to care for his children as well as himself, and that this appropriation can continue after divorce. Custody of children is usually seen as a benefit to women, but it means that they are still doing the work of childcare on their husbands' behalf. A man may pay maintenance towards the children's keep, but the amount paid 'never takes into account the woman's time and work in the material upkeep of the children' (Delphy, 1976b: 82). This is another instance of the lack of relationship between the work done and maintenance received. A divorced woman no longer has to provide personal services to her husband, but as a result she contributes more to the financial costs of the children as well as continuing to care for them. This is not, however, the whole story.

Marriage and divorce can be seen as two ways of achieving the same result: 'the collective attribution to women of the care of children and the collective exemption of men from the same responsibility' (Delphy, 1976b: 85). Delphy proposes that we should consider the institution whereby women assume responsibility for childcare, and the institution whereby individual husbands appropriate wives' labour, as analytically distinct. The 'state of marriage-with-children' can then be seen 'as the meeting place for the two institutions' (1976b: 85). Delphy recognizes that not all children have fathers, in which case caring for them 'is obviously of no benefit to any particular man' (1976b: 86). Furthermore, she doubts whether parents are the only people to benefit from children. Children are, after all, important to the continuity of society as a whole. She suggests that if this is the case, women's responsibility for childcare may be relatively autonomous from the institution of marriage. This does not lead her to the conclusion that childcare is therefore undertaken in the service of capitalism – the analysis favoured by marxist feminists – but to the idea that this institution is another facet of patriarchy. She defines women's responsibility for childcare as 'the collective exploitation of women by men' (1976b: 86). Here her analysis converges with Guillaumin's (1981a), in that women's work is seen as subject to both individual and collective appropriation by men. Delphy argues that the 'individual appropriation of a particular wife's labour by her husband comes over and above this collective appropriation' (1976b: 87). She concludes that this collective appropriation favours marriage. It enables an individual man to make a bargain whereby he undertakes partial responsibility for children – from which he is otherwise exempt – in return for his total appropriation of a wife's unpaid labour.

This analysis in part explains why Delphy has never assumed that women's right to custody of their children is something feminists should defend (Delphy, 1992). There are, however, other reasons why Delphy is wary of advocating maternal rights. In the first place it rests upon assertions of women's 'difference' from (and implicit moral superiority to) men and leads to naturalistic conclusions (see Chapter 5). Second, it reveals women's complicity in maintaining another form of subordination, that of children. Delphy sees the family as founded upon hierarchies of both gender and generation; it is a system in which men dominate women and parents dominate children. Although most of her work has focused on the oppression of women, the place of children as subordinates and dependants has always been recognized in her work. She has pointed out repeatedly that children's unpaid labour can be appropriated by the household head and that children do not consume on equal terms with adults and do not share equally in a family's standard of living. Delphy's long-time collaborator, Diana Leonard, has independently developed this argument in an analysis of childhood (Leonard, 1990b).

In her most recent work Delphy herself has elaborated on this theme in greater detail (1991a, 1992, 1993b, 1994), in response to increasingly vociferous feminist demands for rights over children. She is concerned that many feminists seem to accept the naturalistic and patriarchal assumption that there is a coincidence of interests between children and their mothers and a 'natural' bond between them. Moreover, the specific rights women claim on these grounds are not just rights for women, but rights *over* another category of human beings: children. Feminists assert their rights in children on the grounds that they are less likely to abuse power over them, but, Delphy notes, they rarely consider the fact that an abuse of power can only occur in the presence of power. While feminists have questioned the naturalness and exposed the injustices of men's power over women, they have less often considered that the situation of children may be socially defined rather than naturally given. For Delphy, a feminist project which fails to question 'all forms of subjection, including those which seem natural . . . no longer deserves to be called a liberation project' (1992:19).

In France, as in Britain and the USA, there have been organized attempts on the part of some men to contest the rights of mothers to custody of children. Feminists have understandably opposed what they see as a backlash against women's rights. Delphy, however, is worried about the terms in which feminists claim such rights, the assumption of ownership of children which underlies their unwillingness to share them with men. She raises questions, too, about the derision with which 'new fathers' are treated. Given that feminists have always been critical of traditional male indifference to children, why should they be so negative about some men's attempts to become more involved with childcare? She is, as we might expect, well aware that some of this scepticism about 'new fathers' rests on well-founded suspicions that such men are still not pulling their weight. Nonetheless she suspects that something more is at stake here: 'behind judgements which are perfectly valid *today* . . . i.e. behind the questioning of men's *actual* competence, lurks a radical contesting of their *right* to look after children' (Delphy, 1991a: 113).

Women's claims over children are not, Delphy says, about women's liberation, but about the corporate rights of mothers and are tied to the status of children as private property. Furthermore, if we fail to challenge this we are also failing to question the naturalist ideology which justifies women's subordination:

> Maybe we will end up with full ownership of children; but I don't think this will help children. It won't be much of an improvement for them, even if the new owner proves better than the old one. Nor do I think it will help to liberate women. It may constitute an increase of power for some women *within the gender system as it exists*; but it will be at the

> price of renouncing the perspective of one day obliterating this dividing line: of renouncing the objective of having the gender system disappear. (Delphy, 1992:19; emphasis in original)

Delphy suggests that we need to look more closely at the legal systems which maintain children's subordinate status as 'minors'. This is the subject of her most recent, and as yet unpublished, work (Delphy, 1993b).[13] Here she argues that children, like women, are singled out for special treatment by the law, granted 'exceptional' rights, rights different from those common to all citizens, but at the expense of being excluded from common citizenship rights. The rights accorded to children, such as rights of protection, are not real rights at all – on the contrary they serve to justify other people's rights over them. Rights which are an exception to 'Le droit commun', the law in general, are a means of constituting the private sphere of family relationships as distinct from the public sphere. The public/private dichotomy is thus not natural but a juridical construct. In this private sphere the universalistic legal rights and principles characteristic of the public sphere are suspended.

Where women have made some progress towards gaining universal citizenship rights (see Walby, 1994), children have gained no such rights. Delphy argues that the 'exceptional' rights governing the private sphere accord rights of ownership – of parents over children – which would not be tolerated elsewhere. Delphy offers a number of examples from the French situation to support her argument. For example, parents who abandon their children can assert their 'parental rights' to prevent children being adopted even where they show no interest in them and have no contact with them. Until the United Nations Convention on the Rights of the Child was adopted into French law, a child had no right to legal representation separate from his or her parents. If, for example, a child was abused by her parents she would be represented by the same lawyer who represented the parents. This situation was not remedied until 1993. Even now, children have no absolute right to be heard in decisions concerning where they are to live after their parents' divorce. Children thus lack even the most basic of human rights, such as freedom of movement or freedom to determine where and with whom they should live.

Delphy argues that the group 'children' does not exist as a natural entity, it has no unity except as a legal status. Children are defined as minors under the law, their minority defined in terms of a concept of 'majority' which accords individuals citizenship rights. Although children's status as minors is usually justified on the basis of their assumed 'natural' attributes and capacities, Delphy argues that the notion of a legal 'majority' is purely conventional. In the first place, children are not a homogeneous category, and their social competence varies with their age (see Chapter 5). While this is legally recognized in some contexts, such as when they are granted rights to be heard in court, it is effectively denied by the maintenance of a dichotomy between majority and minority statuses. Moreover, the age of majority is revealed as a convention by the fact that it varies from one nation to another and that within a given nation a child may be considered an adult for some purposes but not for others. For example, children can be tried and punished for a crime, but are denied the right to be represented in court when their parents contest custody over them.

The specific examples Delphy cites come mainly from French law, but similar arguments could be made anywhere in the West. The point she is making is that the legal system serves to perpetuate a family system in which rights of parents over children, like those of men over women, are treated as natural and inevitable. This recent work, then, can be seen as an extension of her analysis of the family as a hierarchical social system. In the next chapter I will return to the issue of women's subordination in order to explain how Delphy's perspective on family relationships leads her to argue that relations between women and men are class relations.

Notes

1. The words 'work' and 'labour' are here being used interchangeably. The French word 'travail' can be translated either as 'work' or as 'labour'. Leonard's translations of Delphy's writings employ the terms synonymously. Marxist feminists, on the other hand, prefer the phrase 'domestic labour'.

2. Delphy's perspective was not considered by participants in this debate. For most of the 1970s her contribution was not widely known outside France and was ignored by many who were aware of it. 'The main enemy' was not translated into

English until 1974 and only became widely available in 1977, but many British marxist feminists knew of this perspective through their participation in the Anglo-French seminar series mentioned in Chapter 1.

3. For summaries of the debate see Malos (1980), Rushton (1979) and Walby (1986a).

4. The concept of the domestic mode of production occupies a central place in Delphy's early work, but receives rather less emphasis in *Familiar Exploitation*, although all the elements of her earlier analysis remain integral to this later work.

5. When Delphy first formulated these ideas, in the early 1970s, this had particular political significance, since establishing the autonomy of feminist struggle from the marxist left was of central importance to the women's movement.

6. Delphy (1978) originally called this 'domestic work'. In the translation published in *Close to Home* (1984) she added a footnote to the effect that 'familial work' was a better term since it captured the crucial importance of the relationship within such work was undertaken.

7. This pattern has been observed in recent British research on dual income families (for example, Brannen and Moss, 1991).

8. Delphy's sole authored work concentrates on women's physical labour within families, occasionally alluding to reproductive labour. In *Familiar Exploitation*, emotional and sexual work are included in the services wives provide for their husbands.

9. Delphy's original insights on differential consumption within households and men's control over it have since been backed by a number of empirical studies (see Brannen and Wilson, 1987; Charles and Kerr, 1988; Graham, 1987; Murcott, 1983; Pahl, 1990).

10. For a quantification of the losses married women incur to their earning power, see Joshi (1987).

11. This move was most evident in Britain in the launch of the journal *m/f* in 1978.

12. The differences between Delphy and Barrett and McIntosh reflect the influence of Althusser's work at this time, particularly his idea that ideology is relatively autonomous from economic relations. This enabled some marxist feminists to study ideological aspects of women's oppression in isolation from its economic aspects – a move Delphy resisted (Delphy, 1981b).

13. The translation of this piece was undertaken by Claire Hadfield.

4

Women as a Class

In examining Delphy's work on economic relationships within families in the last chapter, one crucial element of her argument was omitted: the proposition that women and men constitute opposing classes. This issue deserves a chapter in its own right in order to explain how Delphy arrived at this conclusion and how her analysis of familial relationships challenges much received wisdom about class. As a materialist, she originally formulated her position in relation to marxist theory, but she has also been critical of the way in which class is studied in conventional sociological research (Delphy, 1981c; Delphy and Leonard, 1986). In calling into question much that is taken for granted by both marxists and sociologists, she effectively destabilizes the foundations and boundaries of contemporary theories of class.

Delphy is not alone in viewing relations between men and women in class terms. As we have seen, the idea of women as a class was fundamental to French radical feminism from its earliest days. Feminist theorists elsewhere have also developed analyses of sex-classes, but on a rather different basis. Often it is argued that economic class arises from relations of production while sex-class derives from relations of reproduction. Following this distinction, the American radical feminist Shulamith Firestone asserts that 'sex-class sprang directly from biological reality: men and women were created different, and not equal' (Firestone, 1972: 16). Similarly, some British revolutionary feminists link sex-classes to men's control over women's sexuality and reproductive capacities, but see the origins of this control as social rather than biological. Delphy is critical of such arguments on the grounds that they are naturalistic; even when it is not biology in itself which is held responsible, women's oppression is still reduced to the fact that they have babies (Delphy, [1981b] 1984: 143–4). Like other French materialist feminists, Delphy rejects the relegation of women's subordination to the sphere of reproduction, arguing that it is a specific, exploitative labour relationship which gives rise to the classes 'men' and 'women'.

For many sociologists, marxists and feminists, it is illegitimate to think of men and women as classes. The difficulty is that the term 'class' generally denotes another form of inequality: that deriving from the market economy of capitalist industrial societies. Whether viewed as a product of the relations between capital and wage-labour (as in marxist analysis), or operationalized as an occupational hierarchy (as in most sociological work), class is seen as rooted in the world of paid work outside the domestic sphere. Members of families are generally thought to share a common class location. Feminists are of course aware of inequalities within families and agree that gender divisions cut across class divisions, but most see class and gender as quite different forms of inequality requiring different sorts of explanations. Delphy's methodological procedures, on the other hand, depend on looking for 'what is common to several phenomena of the same order' (Delphy, 1984: 21). She argues that if we stick too closely to what seems specific to women's oppression we lose the ability to see beyond that specificity and deprive ourselves of the tools necessary to locate it in relation to other forms of oppression. For Delphy the subordination of women is one instance of a broader phenomenon, the subordination of one group by another. She therefore thinks it quite legitimate to analyse it through concepts developed in relation to another form of subordination. Part of the appeal of the concept of class for her is precisely that it is not specific to relations between men and women (Delphy, 1984: 25). From this perspective, restricting the term 'class' to inequalities generated in the market economy is to take too narrow a view, one which limits the explanatory potential of a useful concept.

There are other, less contentious, concepts that might be used to describe men and women. They could, for example, simply be called 'groups' but this terminology, says Delphy, tells us nothing about how such groups come into being. The advantage of the concept of class is that it enables us to conceptualize 'men' and 'women' as social categories defined in relation to each other. The term 'groups', on the other hand, tends to imply that such groups already exist as natural entities, prior to any relationship between them, that patterns of domination and subordination are something superimposed upon a natural division. There is then a danger of reducing a social hierarchy to natural causes. This can still happen in some applications of the term 'class' to sexual divisions, as in the position advanced by Firestone (1972). Delphy's usage of the concept of class, however, derives from Marx's insight that classes are social in origin and only come into being through their relationship to each other:

> The concept of class . . . implies that each group cannot be considered separately from the other, because they are bound together by a relationship of domination . . . Characterizing this relationship as one of economic exploitation, the concept of class additionally puts social domination at the heart of the explanation of hierarchy. (Delphy, 1984: 26)

As we shall see in the next chapter, this argument also underpins Delphy's perspective on gender. For now the main point to note is that it is the domination and exploitation of women by men which defines women and men as classes. This is the logical conclusion of her analysis of the domestic mode of production.

Patriarchy and capitalism as two class systems

> Adopting a materialist approach enables us to see and understand the previously unrecognized 'class' relations which exist between men and women. (Delphy and Leonard, 1992: 3)

Class, in the marxist sense, is the product of specific relations of production. Under capitalism the key relations of production are those between capital and wage labour – hence there are two main classes. The bourgeoisie or capitalists own the means of production, while the proletariat or workers make a living by selling their labour-power to the bourgeoisie. Marx did recognize other classes, and marxists disagree among themselves about how to deal with the complexities of the modern class system. There is still, however, a general agreement that the definitive class relations of capitalism are those produced by private ownership of the means of production and the exploitation of the proletariat. This is the only form of class oppression within modern society which most marxists recognize. In extending marxist materialism beyond its original object, Delphy challenges the prevailing view that relations between women and men have no class character.

Since Delphy argues that there are two modes of production existing within modern society, each with its own relations of production and mode of exploitation, it follows that there are two class systems. It is the relations of production of the domestic mode which produce the two classes 'men' and 'women': men are the class of exploiters and women are the exploited class. Within the domestic mode, as we have seen, a woman's unpaid work is appropriated by her husband (or other male kin), whether it be to produce goods or services for exchange or for family consumption. A wife's labour and the products of her labour are not hers to dispose of freely: they are effectively owned by her husband. This is different from the class situation of the 'free' labourer under capitalism who owns his own labour-power and sells it to the capitalist. He is exploited because he does not receive the full value of his labour in exchange: part of it is 'stolen' by the capitalist in the form of surplus value (Delphy and Leonard, 1992: 43). The situation of the husband within patriarchal relations is not exactly the same as that of the capitalist. Capitalists are able to exploit the proletariat because they own the means of production, whereas a husband exploits his wife because he effectively owns her labour, indeed her person: 'Owning the means of production is unnecessary if you own slaves or serfs or wives and children' (Delphy and Leonard, 1992: 43). Whereas capitalism is founded on relations between a property-owning class and a class of wage labourers, patriarchal class relations are based on the direct appropriation of unpaid labour.

A woman is subject to the patriarchal mode of exploitation, to this specific class relation, whether she is the wife of a poor working-class man and her life is one of unremitting toil, or the wife of a prosperous businessman who is freed from physical drudgery in order to concentrate on such wifely duties as planning elaborate dinner parties. The conditions under which wives labour and their standard of living vary enormously, but they share the same location within the relations of domestic production and therefore the same class position within the patriarchal system. It is because this situation is common to almost all women that they constitute a class: 'As a group which is subjected to this relation of production they constitute a class; as a category destined by birth to become members of this class they constitute a caste' (Delphy, 1977a: 16).[1]

As wives women belong to one class, but 'when they participate in capitalist production they enter additionally into a second relation of production', usually as proletarians (1977a: 16). Hence employed women occupy two locations within two distinct modes of production. The same is true of most men: they are exploited as workers within one system and exploit their wives in another. Conventional marxists tend only to consider one of these class systems and therefore try to locate everyone in terms of capitalist relations. This presents a problem since those who do not work within the capitalist system have no class position within it. The usual way of dealing with this in the case of wives is to assign them to the class of their husbands, thus using non-marxist criteria to define their position. As Delphy points out, few women are members of the bourgeoisie in their own right but it is common to hear the phrase 'bourgeois women' used to describe the wives of bourgeois men – as if husbands and wives occupied identical positions. A woman may certainly have a high standard of living by marrying a bourgeois man, but that does not make her a member of that class: 'her standard of living does not depend on her class relationship to the proletariat; but on her serf relations of production to her husband' (Delphy, 1977a: 15). Delphy comments that: 'it is about as accurate to say that the wife of a bourgeois man is herself a bourgeois as it is to say that the slave of a plantation owner is himself a plantation owner' (1977a: 16).

Similarly the term 'working-class woman' can sometimes mean

a woman with a working-class occupation and sometimes a woman married to a man with a working-class job. In the former case she is defined by her position within capitalist labour relations; in the latter case she is simply treated as an appendage to her husband. This usage, common to both marxists and sociologists, is based on the assumption that there is only one class system and conceals the specific position that wives of proletarian or bourgeois men occupy in relation to their husbands.

> By pretending that women belong to their husband's class, the precise fact that wives by definition belong to a class other than that of their husbands is hidden. By pretending that marriage can take the place of relations of production in the capitalist system as the criterion for class membership in this system, the existence of another system of production is masked, and the fact that the relations of production within that system place husbands and wives into two antagonistic classes . . . is hidden. Finally, the 'reintegration' of women into classes by defining them as the property of their husbands has as its objective precisely to hide the fact that they really are the property of their husbands. (Delphy, 1977a: 17)

Delphy's marxist feminist critics often accuse her of using imprecise and non-marxist terminology in discussing class – for example using such terms as slavery, serfdom and caste, with the implication being that she does not understand what class is (see Barrett and McIntosh, 1979: 98; Molyneux, 1979: 13). However, these same critics themselves use non-marxist criteria in contesting the idea that women constitute a class. Frequently the common class location of wives is denied on purely empirical grounds, on the basis that economic differences among women are too great for them to be considered a class. Hence Molyneux, for example, claims that the wife of a bourgeois man does not share the same material oppression as less privileged women, nor does she perform the same domestic chores (1979: 14). This misses the point of Delphy's argument. As Walby notes, a quantitative difference in living standards does not affect the location of wives within patriarchal relations of production. Even if servants are employed, a wife is still dependent on her husband for maintenance in return for managing the household. The level at which a wife is maintained may be relevant in terms of assessing relative standards of living, but it does not affect her class position (Walby,

1986b: 35). Standard of living is not a marxist criteria for determining class, nor is the range of tasks a job entails. No marxist would use such differences among male proletarians to deny that they shared a common class position. One man might undertake skilled work in pleasant, clean conditions for a high rate of pay while another does dirty, menial work for low wages – but both are still proletarians. It is not the tasks one performs, nor the conditions under which one performs them, nor the financial rewards gained, that defines class in marxist terms, but one's location within relations of production.

Objections to Delphy's analysis sometimes simply take the form of reasserting the common class position of household members. Olivia Harris, for example, takes Delphy to task for treating all women as occupying the same location within the domestic mode of production irrespective of 'the class position of the household in which their lives are constructed' (Harris, 1981: 58). In statements like this the possibility of class divisions within families is denied: 'class position' means the class deriving from the capitalist system. When differences among women are invoked, as they are by Molyneux, these boil down to differences defined by virtue of women's husbands' position in the class system. Delphy has often drawn attention to a paradox at the heart of such arguments, that class differences between women are asserted on the basis of what is being denied: their common location as men's dependants.

> The differences between the wives (or cohabitees or daughters) of middle class men and the wives (or cohabitees or daughters) of working class men is based . . . on the class relationship they have in common: their relationship with a husband/father. They are all defined by the men to whom they are related. (Delphy and Leonard, 1992: 69)

Differences among women: class politics and the politics of class

Delphy has been criticized for 'ignoring the very real class divisions between women' (Barrett and McIntosh, 1979: 101). She does not, however, deny that differences among women exist and are materially important, nor does she ignore the existence of other systematic systems of inequality. The implication of her position is that in modern societies several such systems intersect, hence an individual may be differently located within each of these. Asserting that women are a class does not negate the privileges that, say, a white middle-class career woman has relative to other women. Delphy has tended to focus primarily on only two dimensions of inequality. She does not give systematic attention to the specific, racialized oppressions that black women and other women of colour face, although she does raise the issue of racism from time to time. She has, however, shown herself to be acutely aware of the relative privileges that some women, including herself, enjoy and is explicitly critical of those who use the common oppression of women to deny other oppressions.

> Some think that being women we are only women, and hence absolved by our quality of victims in this regard from our privileges in any other. But we materialist feminists, who affirm the existence of several – at least two – class systems, and hence the possibility of an individual having several class memberships (which can in addition be contradictory); we who think that male workers are not, as victims of capitalism, thereby absolved of the sin of being the beneficiaries of patriarchy, must refuse this way out. (Delphy, [1980b] 1984: 147)

Feminists today are accustomed to talking about differences among women, the complex intersections between gender, class, sexuality, 'race', nationality and so on, which shape women's lives. This was not, however, what was at stake for Delphy's marxist feminist critics. Rather they were in the business of arguing for the pre-eminence of one form of oppression – that of the capitalist class system – over all others. Hence socialist feminists, both activists and theorists, have tended to concentrate on the situation of working-class women. This meant ignoring middle-class or 'bourgeois' women and often involved denying that such women could be oppressed. Even when dealing with working-class women, such women have often been defined as wives of male proletarians and their oppression analysed as contributing to the oppression of their men. This was true, for example, of the logic underpinning the domestic labour debate where women's work was seen as useful to capitalism because it 'reproduces' more (male) labour-power to be exploited. Delphy and Leonard argue that women are thus treated as if they are not 'worth oppressing in and of themselves' but only insofar as their oppression 'furthers the exploitation of proletarian men' (1992: 34).

Delphy has always insisted that each system of inequality or oppression should be analysed independently, not as a by-product of some other system of oppression. To see women as a class means accepting that their oppression is as serious as that of the male proletariat, and this disrupts the usual ordering of priorities among both left activists and marxist theorists. When 'class' was raised in the early years of the women's movement, it was usually a means of denying an oppression common to all women and reasserting the primacy of the class struggle against capitalism. Because this class system was seen as the only one that mattered, women deemed privileged within it – even if only by virtue of the men they were married to – were excluded from the ranks of the oppressed. 'Bourgeois' women were branded as 'class enemies', they were 'the favourite target of male "revolutionaries"' (Delphy, [1977b] 1984: 121).[2] Delphy points out that bourgeois women are few in number, that they have never rushed to join the women's movement, yet they were constantly invoked as a threat to that movement and used to undermine its claims to represent women as a whole. They were, she argues, largely mythical creations, for which particular individuals – in France, Madame Pompidou, in the USA, Jackie Kennedy – stood as 'symbols' (Delphy, 1984: 121).

This point has been misunderstood. Barrett and McIntosh say that Delphy 'roundly defends her solidarity with the wives of prominent men' (1979: 101), but this was not her intention. Rather she wished to uncover what lay beneath this vilification of bourgeois women, to explore what individuals like Madame Pompidou or Jackie Kennedy symbolized. This is not a matter of defending privileged women, but of examining what hostility to them tells us about traditional class politics. She believes it reveals a deep misogyny among left men, and complex feelings of guilt and unworthiness among left women. This is the argument which she develops at length in 'Our friends and ourselves' (1977b, 1984).

Delphy sees men's attitudes to bourgeois women as a displacement of hatred of bourgeois men onto their wives. What is interesting is that greater venom is often directed at these women than at the real 'class enemy' – their husbands. Why should this be? Delphy suggests two explanations. First, such women are seen as the property of men, hence attacks on them are a threat to the property rights of the bourgeoisie, their exclusive access to their women. Second, these women are seen as having illegitimate privileges which place them in positions above some men, hence they are 'out of their rightful place', they are 'usurpers' (Delphy, 1984: 123). Delphy suggests that insults – especially in the form of sexual threats – directed at such women reveal the opposite of what they claim to express. They are not provoked by class consciousness in the usual sense, but by indignation at *women* wielding any power or influence. Hence putting such women in their place – as subordinate to men – has been a favourite subject for cartoons in the left press and for stories of masculine bravado.[3] In this context Delphy gives considerable attention to Claude Alzon, a French male sociologist who wrote extensively on women's issues. Alzon criticizes bourgeois women as idle parasites who exploit their husbands, and likens them to prostitutes whom he sees as exploiting their clients. This reversal of what feminists would see as the actual power relations between men and women is revealing. He is effectively saying 'those women to whom I have no access, those whom I cannot oppress, they are tarts just like the rest!' (Delphy, [1977b] 1984: 127). This sort of thinking, says Delphy, reveals a hatred of all women, that women are only acceptable when they know their place.

How are we to account for women taking on similar attitudes? The picture here is complicated by the way in which the term 'bourgeois' is used in left circles. Sometimes it denotes the real bourgeoisie or capitalists, those who own a substantial stake in the means of production, but often it is extended to cover the middle class.[4] Now most activists and theorists on the left are 'bourgeois' in the latter sense: they are not manual workers and hence not part of the proletariat they claim to represent. Delphy argues that left women 'share with their men the guilt of having class privileges', but this is exacerbated by 'the guilt of having these privileges improperly, being "women"' (1984: 131). It is this guilt which is then displaced onto 'bourgeois' women whom socialist women simultaneously identify with and distance themselves from. Hence only 'working-class women' – often meaning the wives of working-class men – are seen as truly oppressed. Delphy sees this stance as deriving from 'self-hatred' because they define themselves as bourgeois, 'false consciousness' since they believe that they possess the same privileges as their men, and a 'guilty conscience' derived from the feeling that they usurp whatever privileges they have: 'Not content with feeling themselves *particularly unworthy of oppressing others*, left women feel themselves *unworthy of being oppressed*' (Delphy, 1984: 132; emphasis in original). They are thus unable to put their own oppression on the same footing as class or racial oppression.

> Why? Because the 'working class' (but also the 'Blacks') are represented by *men*, and images show them in particularly 'virile' attitudes: wearing helmets, armed and shaking their fists. This image is the one with the highest status for revolutionary women. (Delphy, 1984: 132)

This imagery is still prevalent among sections of the revolutionary left and will be familiar to anyone who has ever been involved in left politics. Delphy goes on:

> To think of yourself as a class is primarily to think of yourself as a *man*, and, furthermore, to think of yourself as a man of the most *glorious* category. It is to raise yourself to the rank of the cultural heroes . . . this is unthinkable for the majority of women. It would be a double sacrilege, a double profanity: it would defame the dignity of men and the dignity of the proletariat. (1984: 132–3; emphasis in original)

The form of politics which declared the primacy of the class struggle over women's oppression, then, is seen by Delphy as deriving from the derogation of women. A working-class woman's oppression is seen as secondary to that of her husband; he is the real hero of the struggle against capitalist oppression and her class position is defined as an adjunct to his. The 'bourgeois woman' is scapegoated because she is seen as usurping her position precisely because, being a woman, she is not really bourgeois – and has no business being bourgeois. 'Bourgeois' women owe 'their "class position", which is held to outweigh their status as women, to this very gender-status' (Delphy, 1984: 135). Attitudes to bourgeois women are of interest because they bring into the open the hidden substratum of those arguments which stress the primacy of class.

> Hostility towards 'bourgeois women' . . . rests, in the final analysis, on the correct perception that women do not really belong to the bourgeois class. This hostility reveals that gender membership, an individual's patriarchal class, is perceived as outweighing, and furthermore as rightly outweighing, their 'class' membership. (Delphy, 1984: 135–6)

Delphy concludes that it is as *women* that bourgeois women are vilified. Bourgeois women are thus seen as having no right to their privileges, because they derive them from their men. Similarly working-class women are seen as having no right to be independently oppressed: their oppression derives from that of their men. The very analyses that deny women's common class position rely on that class position – their common dependence on men – in order to deny it. This paradox is not only to be found among the left, but also in conventional sociological analyses of class.

Sociological perspectives on class and stratification

Sociologists use the term 'social stratification' to denote systematic inequalities which persist over time and which result in the emergence of hierarchically ranked social groups or 'strata'. Although the concept of 'stratification' can be applied to any form of persistent social inequality, in practice most sociologists – especially in Britain and Europe – have concentrated on class inequality, the inequality generated by divisions of labour within the market economy. Racism and gender inequality have only recently, and sometimes grudgingly, been accepted as aspects of stratification at all. Class still tends to be treated as *the* system of stratification so that other forms of inequality are regarded as less central to the structure of society: 'One form of hierarchy is . . . not only the most studied, it has the linguistic right to be *the* social hierarchy' (Delphy and Leonard, 1986: 60).

Moreover, women are often ignored or rendered invisible in studies of class because the family is usually taken to be the unit of stratification. The location of a family within the class structure is then determined by the occupation of its (usually male) head and other family members are held to share his class position. Delphy and Leonard suggest that sociologists use the term 'class' in two senses. On the one hand it refers to the collectivity of individuals who hold positions within the capitalist division of labour. On the other hand it is used to encompass the social milieu of those individuals, and includes their dependants. Applying the same term to these different groups, the first of which is much smaller than the second, confuses the two.

> It also hides the fact that the individuals who are 'in' a class but who do not occupy the positions which define the class, find themselves in a very different position from those who do. The problem of 'non-holders' of positions – who they are and what their status is within the class – thus remains largely unbroached by sociology. (Delphy and Leonard, 1986: 58)

Different locations within families have often been understood simply as 'roles' rather than positions within a hierarchical structure. Even now, when inequalities within families have been subjected to more serious scrutiny, they are not seen in class terms. Class is thought of in terms of inequalities between families rather than inequalities within them. This is, as Delphy (1981c) says, another instance of treating the family as an undifferentiated unit, thus disguising inequalities within it. Wives are assumed to occupy the same place in the class hierarchy as their husbands, implying an equality between spouses that does not exist.

Sociologists' inability to see the differences between holders and non-holders of class positions derives from similar preoccupations to those underlying class politics. Like left activists, they are primarily interested in divisions and conflicts between men. Their thinking on class is dictated by what Delphy and Leonard call a 'patriarchal chain of reasoning' (1986: 59). This chain is circular and rests on the presumption that only one form of class inequality is of real social significance. Sociologists are concerned primarily with male proletarian oppression, therefore they focus on the capitalist wage-labour system of the market economy; therefore they define market capitalism or the occupational hierarchy as *the* system of inequalities; therefore they see these inequalities and this system as determining everything else and hence they can assert the primacy of 'class' oppression as they define it.

There are now numerous critiques of the treatment of women in stratification theory and research. In particular, the practice of ignoring the occupational class of employed wives and ranking families by the occupation of their head has been questioned (see Acker, 1980; Crompton and Mann, 1986; Roberts, 1993; Stanworth, 1984). Some, however, continue to defend the conventional view (see, for example, Goldthorpe 1983, 1984). Most of those objecting to sociologists' gender blinkeredness have concentrated on women's paid employment, suggesting that as most married women are now employed they should, where possible, be classified according to their own occupations. It is also argued that women's independent class position has an impact on their families and should therefore be taken into account in classifying families by class (Britten and Heath, 1983; Stanworth, 1984). These newer perspectives, however, have still not resolved 'the issue of what to do with non-holders' of class positions (Delphy and Leonard, 1986: 61), in particular wives who are not employed. Sylvia Walby, from a perspective informed by Delphy's work, similarly argues that attempts to revise approaches to class do not go far enough. They are still working within a 'male-centred problematic' which does not give sufficient conceptual space to inequalities within families. What is needed, she argues, is 'a rethinking of the central questions of stratification theory' (Walby, 1986b: 30). This is something which Delphy's work provides.

Delphy's 'Women in stratification studies', first published in France in 1977, was an early contribution to feminist debates on this issue. It remains a radical challenge to the ways in which sociologists think about class. Delphy was not the first to point out the androcentric bias of sociological research in this area and she drew on earlier work, particularly that of Joan Acker (1973), in developing her own argument. Acker was among the few who suggested that housewives might be treated as an occupational category. This, however, she saw as a way of integrating women without paid work into a broader ranking of occupational class. Delphy has gone further in positing a separate class *system* in which wives occupy a specific class position in relation to their husbands, rather than simply a location within a wider, more general, social hierarchy. This, she suggests, is the only way of dealing with inconsistencies which arise in trying to incorporate women into existing models of class stratification (1977a, 1981c).

One such inconsistency, now widely acknowledged to be problematic, is the practice of classifying single women by their own occupation but assigning married women to the class of their husbands. Behind the double standard applied to single and married women is a further double standard which is less often noted: 'Occupation, the universal measure of an individual's social class is, in the case of women, and only of women, replaced by a completely different criterion – marriage' (Delphy, [1981c] 1984: 29). According to Delphy, this leads to the major contradiction in studies of social stratification, 'that women are not integrated into the description of the social structure by applying a rule governing the concept of social stratification, but rather by abandoning this rule' ([1981c] 1984: 29). Hence sociologists incorporate women into their accounts of social class by ignoring their usual general principles. She illustrates these points through a detailed consideration of two major French research projects. For reasons of space I will consider only one of these: a study of self-employed workers which Delphy herself participated in.[5]

One aspect of this research was a comparison of the background and current positions of husbands and wives and the siblings (brothers and sisters) of both spouses. In particular, the researchers were interested in the relative social mobility (movement up or down the class hierarchy) of siblings. All of the respondents were married; 90 per cent were male and 10 per cent were female. *All* the men included in the study – whether as respondents, or as spouses, or brothers (or brothers-in-law) of the respondents – were classified by their own occupations. The criteria for classifying women were less consistent: women respondents, wives of respondents, and sisters (or sisters-in-law), were all treated differently. Nor was marriage the sole criterion for this different treatment. The women included in the study in their own right (10 per cent of the sample and, remember, all married) were classified by their occupation. Wives of male respondents were classified by two alternative criteria: their own job if they were in paid employment, but by their husband's job if they were not. A different distinction was applied to the sisters (and sisters-in-law) of respondents – whether or not they were married. 'Their class position was determined by *their* occupation if they were single, but by their *husbands*' occupation if they were married' ([1981c] 1984: 31). Thus while men were judged by only one criteria – their own occupation, women were judged by two – their own occupation or their husbands' – and not all women were judged by the same two criteria. Some employed married women were thus classified by their own occupation – like single women – whereas other employed married women were classified by their husbands' occupations. If this seems ridiculously complex, it becomes even more bizarre when we consider what this study was trying to achieve.

It would be confusing enough if the study were simply classifying individual class positions but, since its purpose was to compare the class position of siblings, the confusion is compounded. The position of the women in the original couples was determined *either* by their own occupation (if they were employed *or* if they were the original, self-employed, respondents) *or* their husbands' occupation (if they were not employed *and* not the original respondents). They were compared first with their brothers (classified by their own occupation), second with their single sisters (classified by their own occupation) and third with their married sisters (classified by their husbands' occupation, irrespective of whether or not they were employed). As Delphy comments, calculations arrived at in this way can hardly be meaningful since they do not compare like with like.

Most feminist sociologists would argue that all the women studied should have been treated consistently and classified by their occupations – if they had one – irrespective of their marital status. This common solution to such problems would certainly simplify matters but it would not satisfy Delphy, since it implies that if a married woman has no occupation it is quite legitimate to assign her to her husband's class. There is still a double standard in operation, with men being classified only by their own occupations but some women – those without paid jobs – being classified by their husbands' occupations. This raises more general issues about how women become included in social classes for purposes of sociological research. In particular, Delphy questions the practice of defining women as members of the same class as the men they are dependent upon. She argues that assigning women with paid jobs to an occupational class in their own right, while leaving those without an occupation in the class of their husbands, does not solve the problem – indeed it amplifies the confusion around women's class position: 'In systematically attributing to a woman without an occupation the occupation of her husband, an essentially dichotomous variable – that of the presence or absence of economic independence – is ignored' (Delphy, [1981c] 1984: 36).

A married woman with a paid job, which is usually of a lower status than that of her husband, will be placed in a different, lower, class than she would occupy if she had no occupation. Hence an employed woman 'is considered to be more distanced socially from her husband than a woman who does not work outside the home' (Delphy, 1984: 36). This is clearly an absurdity:

> The fact that a woman is comparable to her husband from the point of view of economic independence distances her from him in sociological terms. Putting a non-employed woman into her husband's social class does not just obscure this fact, it completely reverses its meaning. (Delphy, 1984: 36)

There is obviously something amiss with conventional sociological procedures when they lead to such illogical conclusions. The problem, for Delphy, lies in the uncritical use of the criterion of association by marriage, which is alien to the normal way of establishing class membership through occupation. The usual criticism of stratification studies – that they ignore the occupational class of married women with jobs – assumes that only those with an occupation have an independent class position. The corollary of this is that those without an occupation have no real place in the social structure, no social existence. If we do not accept this then we must, says Delphy, conclude that married women without occupations *do* occupy a specific position. It is not enough to deny the validity of assigning women with jobs to their husbands' class: we must extend this criticism to cover all married women. As things stand, the specific position of married women without an occupation is not taken into account, but nor are they considered as having no class position. Instead they are placed in someone else's class.

In practice, as Delphy notes, many studies of stratification deal only with the occupational distribution of men or, at best, with the 'economically active' population (married women without paid jobs are defined as 'economically inactive'). As operationalized for research purposes, social classes thus contain few or no women. Yet the concept of class as a system of stratification is supposed to cover all the population: we are all members of classes. In fact, using occupation as the sole criterion of class membership excludes the majority of the population – those past retirement age, women, children and other dependants— who are not 'holders' of class positions in their own right (Delphy and Leonard, 1986). The problems this raises are rarely confronted by sociologists. Women, the most permanent non-holders of class positions within conventional sociological definitions, are dealt with by introducing a specific criterion which applies only to them: marriage. Women, sometimes as daughters as well as wives, are assumed to have only indirect class membership mediated through their husbands or fathers.

Married women without occupations clearly do have only an indirect and mediated relationship with the labour market. Delphy has no quarrel with this interpretation of women's situation, only with the way it is used by sociologists to obscure what it should illuminate – the specific economic position of married women. Such women, whether or not they are in paid employment, do have a relationship to production but within a separate mode of production distinct from that of capitalism. Conventional sociology, however, deals only with the classes rooted in the system of wage-labour. In using marriage as a criterion for establishing the class position of women without recognizing it as a labour relationship, sociology produces a distorted picture of women's socio-economic position.

The specific relations of production within which married women are located are characterized by dependence. Sociologists use the fact of this dependence as the basis for placing women in the same class as their husbands. They then, as Delphy says, conveniently forget this and assume parity of status between husbands and wives. The supposedly shared social class of spouses is thought to override any inequality between them. Inequality between men and women is then defined as of secondary importance, as less socially significant than the inequalities resulting from the occupational class system. Such arguments rest on an assumed *equal* status of spouses which is in turn based on women's dependence and hence on the *inequality* between spouses. Hence Delphy argues that the actual situation is the reverse of that claimed by sociologists:

> Not only do the relations of production which put husband and wife into patriarchal and antagonistic classes override the commonality of industrial class, since they precede it both chronologically and logically, but they contradict it, since women without an occupation are by definition outside the industrial class system. (Delphy, 1984: 39)

Even when women have an occupation and therefore are classifiable in terms of the industrial class system, sociologists still often put them in their husbands' class which, Delphy suggests, constitutes a tacit acceptance of the pre-eminence of patriarchal relations. The fact of women's dependence ought to reveal their true class situation, but is used by sociologists to obscure it. Sociology roots its analysis in women's dependence, in 'the specific antagonistic relations of production between husbands and wives' but then 'not only denies this relationship, but turns it into its very opposite: a relationship of equals' (Delphy, 1984: 39).

The problem of bringing women into class analysis, then, is underpinned by sociologists' reluctance to see family relations as fully social and hierarchical. Those who continue to defend the conventional sociological view can thus, like Goldthorpe, claim that 'the class position of the conjugal family should be seen as unitary' (1984: 497). Delphy and Leonard (1986) draw attention to the ways in which this view blinkers sociologists to the inequalities in work, consumption and inheritance which were discussed in the last chapter. Because sociologists fail to consider the internal workings of families in their class analysis, they see only different 'roles' rather than a hierarchically ordered division of labour and rewards. When they study the transmission of class positions from one generation to the next, or mobility between class positions, they fail to notice the differences between the life patterns of male and female children or even older sons and younger sons. Social mobility studies are supposed to give us a picture of the degree of fluidity or rigidity in the class system, but they fail to consider how processes going on within families contribute to mobility or the lack of it. They do not consider how these processes can result in the dispersal of members of one family of origin to different class locations. Delphy and Leonard conclude that the lack of attention to divisions within families restricts the scope of sociological analysis and distorts analyses of the reproduction of the social structure over time.

Are women a class or only wives?

Although her argument for women being a class centres on the labour relationship of marriage, Delphy can be read as implying that 'women' and 'men' as social categories – and not just husbands and wives – can be considered as social classes. This reading derives from her assertion of the normality of marriage as a social position for women: that it is the assumed destiny of all women to become wives, and that this affects all of us, whether or not we marry (Delphy, 1977a, 1980b). Sylvia Walby reads Delphy in this way and argues, against the position she imputes to Delphy, that while housewives and husbands constitute two classes, women and men as such do not (Walby, 1986b).

Walby, as we have seen, views Delphy's work as a means of reshaping class theory. She follows Delphy in arguing for the coexistence of two modes of production, capitalist and patriarchal (see Chapter 3), and therefore accepts the premise that each is the foundation for a separate class system. She argues that housewives, whether or not they are also employed, are a class exploited by their husbands, who are also a class. Like Delphy she notes that women who are employed have a dual location within each of the two class systems. She explains her apparent differences with Delphy as follows:

> I do not believe that it is appropriate to designate all women as a class. Not all women are housewives, and thus not all women have a class position within the patriarchal mode of production. This applies only to those women who perform unpaid domestic labour for a husband (or father) in a household and not all women are in this position. It is not appropriate to accord to all women a common class position on the

> basis that most women will expect, at some point in their lives, to be housewives. (Walby, 1986b: 35)

Walby probably overstates her disagreement with Delphy here. Delphy would see women and men as classes in the strict sense of the term only within the domestic mode of production, hence her early usage of such terms as status and caste when talking about women in general.[6]

Walby goes on to argue that an individual's class position should be assessed solely on the basis of their own location within economic relations. While there are numerous other forms of oppression common to all women, relating to sexuality, violence, discrimination in the workplace and so on, these cannot accurately be described as part of a class situation. Her reasoning here is that these forms of oppression are not directly derived from a shared economic position, and that it would stretch the concept of class too far to see them as aspects of a class situation. She suggests an alternative which would recognize that some of the ways in which men and women are ranked hierarchically are relatively autonomous from economic relations: the Weberian term 'status groups'. Hence, for Walby, wives and husbands are classes, but women and men are status groups. From a materialist perspective, I would argue, this distinction is problematic.

Max Weber used the term 'status', as opposed to class, to denote ranked evaluations of social honour or prestige. Certainly women have less 'status' than men in this sense, but are we only dealing here with an evaluation of women's worth or something more concrete? For example, it is surely not only an evaluation of women's lesser prestige that leads men to defend patriarchal privilege in the workplace. As Walby has herself argued elsewhere (1986a), this is a matter of men's material interests. Furthermore, the concept of 'status' can be invoked from a naturalistic perspective to suggest that the problem is not material inequalities between women and men, but rather the undervaluing of womanly characteristics – a position Delphy rigorously opposes (1976a, 1987a). Delphy sometimes uses the term 'status' in a descriptive sense, but prefers 'class' as an analytical tool precisely because it emphasizes the social origins of gender hierarchy. She says that class 'is the only concept I know which at least partially responds to the strict requirements of a *social* explanation' (1984: 25). It focuses attention on women and men as social categories defined by the material inequalities between them, rather than as natural groups which happen to be differentially valued. Here, however, Delphy is using class in a rather different, and broader, sense than when referring to the classes deriving from the domestic mode of production.

Talking of women and men as a whole as classes does cast the concept of class adrift from its moorings in specific relations of production. To this extent Walby's misgivings have some foundation. Even deprived of this sure anchorage, however, the advantage of 'class' as a concept is that it denotes material oppression. It should be remembered that Delphy's materialism emphasizes social practice. It is not economically reductionist: she does not see the economy as determining all else, rather the economy is itself the result of social practices, of specific social relations. Extending the concept of class beyond the bounds of specific productive relations may horrify marxist purists, but a materialist case for it can still be made.

In the introduction to *Close to Home*, Delphy uses the term class in its strict sense, as deriving from the domestic mode of production, and, more tentatively, to refer to the structural division between the sexes more generally. The latter may still be seen as materialist in that men and women are defined in relation to each other, within institutionalized hierarchies, as dominant and dominated 'classes'. Other materialist feminists have suggested wider foundations for the class relation between men and women. Guillaumin (1981a), for example, suggests that it is based on the individual and collective appropriation of women and their labour, while Wittig (1992) locates it in institutionalized heterosexuality. In *Familiar Exploitation*, Delphy and Leonard themselves suggest that class relations between women and men may be characteristic of the world of paid work and unpaid work:

> we are moving towards an understanding of the gender constitution of classes and the class constitution of gender, recognizing that within both the domestic and the capitalist modes of production men and women constitute opposed classes or class fractions, in that men (as fathers and husbands, and employers and privileged male workers) directly benefit from the oppression/exploitation of women's work. (Delphy and Leonard, 1992: 160)

If we accept that men and women are classes, there are still times when we wish to refer to class in its conventional sense and to differentiate this from gender classes. We may want to discuss the relationship between the two hierarchies, as in the above quote from Delphy and Leonard. In these cases we find ourselves falling back on other concepts, such as gender. Elsewhere in *Familiar Exploitation*, Delphy and Leonard use the formulation 'class like' or place the term 'class' in inverted commas, suggesting some ambivalence about the term (1992: 3, 258). So defining women as a class can sometimes be confusing, but it is no more confusing than conventional marxist and sociological practices which define women in terms of their husbands' or fathers' class. Until we have another term which captures the social and material bases of the hierarchy between men and women, materialist feminists are likely to concur with Delphy when she says that the concept of class 'is perhaps not totally satisfactory, but it is the least unsatisfactory of all the terms used to analyse oppression' (1984: 25).

Notes

1. In this context Delphy uses the term class in relation to the situation of women working within the domestic mode of production and caste to describe the category women as a whole. Her use of the term 'caste' is confined to 'The main enemy'. The issue of whether it is appropriate to extend the term class to women as a whole is one to which I return later in the chapter.
2. These views continue to have some salience among some sections of the left (see, for example, Petty et al., 1987).
3. They may feel even more need to use these tactics when a woman is powerful in their own right. For example at a demonstration against the British Conservative government in the early 1980s, at which I was present, there were placards featuring a photograph of the Prime Minister, Margaret Thatcher, with the caption 'Wanted for Rape'. Several men had made a handwritten addition: 'and I'm the man to do it'. That opposition to a right-wing head of government took this sexist form is an illustration of the attitudes Delphy is critical of.
4. This is especially so where women are concerned (see Petty et al., 1987).
5. This was a project Delphy was involved in as a research assistant in her early years at CNRS. She would not have had responsibility for designing the research.
6. Delphy, personal correspondence.

5

The Question of Gender

The concept of gender is used by feminists to emphasize the social shaping of femininity and masculinity – to challenge the idea that relations between women and men are ordained by 'nature'. The term is most commonly employed among English speakers and has seldom been adopted in France (see Delphy, 1993a; Haraway, 1991). Delphy is unusual among French feminists in preferring the word 'gender' over 'sex'. The latter, she feels, cannot easily be divested of its naturalistic connotations and is therefore less suited to materialist analysis (Delphy, 1984, 1993a). As a materialist feminist, Delphy is opposed to the notion that current social arrangements are in any way 'natural' (see Chapters 1 and 2). From this perspective, 'women' and 'men' are not biological categories, but social ones. In this chapter I will explain Delphy's ideas on gender, outline their evolution in her work and show how they fit into her overall theoretical framework. First, however, it is necessary to place the materialist feminist position in the context of wider feminist debates around gender and sexual difference.

In recent years the concept of gender has been called into question as part of ongoing debates on essentialism and constructionism. The way in which the concept was originally formulated, in relation to biological sex, has proved something of a problem. Generally a distinction is made between 'sex' as the biological differences between male and female and 'gender' as a cultural distinction between masculinity and femininity (see Oakley, 1972: 16). There have always been some feminists who disliked this distinction. Psychoanalytic theorists maintain that sex, gender and sexuality are inextricably linked and cannot be disentangled from each other (Adams, 1989; Mitchell, 1982). This is the case both for those psychoanalysts who see femininity and masculinity as culturally constructed and for those who assume that some essential difference exists prior to cultural influences. Feminists interested in asserting women's 'difference' – whether from a psychoanalytic perspective or not – often object to the sex–gender distinction because they see it as denying the specificity of women's bodily experience (Brodribb, 1992; Irigaray, 1985, 1993). This is a tendency which has long been strong in France and is beginning to gain ground elsewhere.

On the other hand there are those who reject the sex–gender distinction on the grounds that its challenge to essentialism does not go far enough: it still assumes a natural sex on to which gender is grafted. Hence it is argued that we should question the very existence of gender categories themselves and ask why and how the social world is divided into the two groups we call 'women' and 'men'. This position is often associated with recent writings by poststructuralists and postmodernists, such as Butler (1990), Davies (1989) and Riley (1988), but it began to be developed by French radical feminists in the 1970s.[1] It was, for example, identified as a central principle of radical feminism in the editorial to the first issue of *Questions Féministes* in 1977. Materialist radical feminists, however, differ from poststructuralists and postmodernists in one very crucial respect. The latter see the meaning of social categories as fluid and shifting, constantly being contested and renegotiated. Materialists, while accepting that these categories can and must be challenged, see them as rooted in social practices and structural inequalities which are built into the fabric of society. This difference in perspective is an important one. Postmodernists deny the material reality of gender categories and play down the ways in which they constrain us. For Delphy and her associates, these categories may be socially constructed, but they are nonetheless a real, material fact of (social) life. This is because 'men' and 'women' are not abstract categories constructed merely through language or discourse, but are founded upon unequal, exploitative, material relationships – in short, class relationships.

Hierarchy and division

Delphy's position on gender follows from her conceptualization of men and women as classes and is thus rooted in the fundamental assumptions of French radical feminism. If relations between women and men are class relations, then gender divisions have nothing to do with nature but are the product of social and economic structures. Patriarchal domination is not based upon pre-existing sex differences; rather gender exists as a social division because of patriarchal domination. Hence hierarchy precedes division. As Delphy and Leonard put it:

> For us 'men' and 'women' are not two naturally given groups who at some time fell into a hierarchical relationship. Rather the reason the two groups are distinguished socially is because one dominates the other in order to use its labour. In other words, it is the relationship of production which produces the two classes 'men' and 'women'. (1992: 258)

This argument is in keeping with a marxist method of analysis. For marxists classes only exist in relation to one another, so, for example, there can be no bourgeoisie without the proletariat and vice versa. Capitalists could not exist without proletarians to work for them and produce wealth; workers could not survive without capitalists to employ them. At a conceptual level, the bourgeois class is defined by its exploitation of the proletariat's labour-power and the proletariat by selling its labour-power to capital. Similarly 'men' and 'women' exist as socially significant categories because of the exploitative relationship which both binds them together and sets them apart from each other. Conceptually, there could be no 'women' without the opposing category 'men', and vice versa.

Because they analysed women's oppression in terms of class, French radical feminists emphasized the social aspect of sex categories. From the 1970s they began to speak of social men and social women as distinct from biological males and females (see, for example, Delphy, 1975, 1976a; Guillaumin, 1987; Mathieu, 1977; Wittig, 1982). Since they argued that the existence of men and women as social groups, as classes, was founded on unequal, exploitative relationships, they were critical of both biologistic and psychologistic explanations of sex difference. Femininity and masculinity could not be understood simply as psychological differences between women and men, but were related to their respective material situations. Hence in 'For a materialist feminism' (published in *L'Arc* in 1975) Delphy objects to psychoanalysis on the grounds that it is a form of idealism, that it treats subjectivity and sexuality as outside material social relations. Attempts to reconcile psychoanalysis and marxism therefore undermine the materialism of the latter.

The beginnings of a materialist conception of gender are evident in 'Protofeminism and antifeminism', published in 1976, in which Delphy attacks the naturalistic premises of Annie Leclerc's *Parole de femme* (1974). While focusing on this one work, as I discussed earlier, Delphy makes it clear that she is taking it as exemplary of a particular tendency within French feminist thought: that which takes women's 'difference' as its starting point. In challenging this notion of intrinsic difference, she introduces some key tenets of her emerging perspective on gender. As was explained in Chapter 2, the central problem as Leclerc sees it is the devaluation of women within our culture. She views men and women as embodying different values, arising from their respective relation to biological reproduction. Like many feminists writing in the 1970s, Delphy was concerned to challenge the biologistic assumptions underpinning arguments of this kind. At that time feminists sought to demonstrate that the attributes we deem feminine and masculine, along with the sexual division of labour, vary cross-culturally and historically (see, for example, Oakley, 1972). The content of gender categories was thus revealed as social rather than natural. Delphy, along with other French radical feminists, began to take this a stage further, to argue that the categories themselves, and not just their content, were social. In other words the terms 'men' and 'women' describe social groups not natural entities, groups defined by the hierarchical relationship between them. This is fundamental to her critique of Leclerc. Leclerc's argument, says Delphy, is couched in the terms of the dominant ideology because it assumes first that 'men and women as they are today . . . are given, if not natural, entities' and second that hierarchy 'came after and independent of these divisions' (Delphy, 1984: 183). Hence Leclerc perpetuates 'our society's general confusion of biological males and females and the social categories of men and women' (1984: 184). At this point, however, the radical implications of treating 'men' and 'women' as social categories were not yet fully elaborated.

This was soon to be remedied. A year after the publication of 'Protofeminism', the journal *Questions Féministes* was launched and its lead article, collectively written by the editors, spelled out their position on sex differences in some detail. In a section which Delphy co-authored with Monique Plaza, they argue that opposition to naturalistic explanations of sexual difference is a basic tenet of radical feminism. Women's oppression derives from a patriarchal social system and 'in order to describe and unmask this oppression, arguments that have recourse to "nature" must be shattered' (*Questions Féministes* Collective, [1977] 1981: 214). Ideas of feminine difference embraced by the 'neo-femininity' current of French feminism derive from the patriarchal system – which uses the idea of difference to justify and conceal our exploitation. To counter this ideology, they argue, radical feminism must refuse any notion of 'woman' that is unrelated to social context. The next step in this argument is a crucial one.

> The corollary of this refusal is our effort to deconstruct the notion of 'sex differences' which gives a shape and a base to the concept of 'woman' and is an integral part of naturalist ideology. The social mode of being of men and of women is in no way linked to their nature as males and females nor with the shape of their sex organs. (1981: 214–15)

The implications of this are indeed radical. The political goal envisaged is not the raising of women's status, nor equality between women and men, but the abolition of sex differences themselves. In a non-patriarchal society there would be no social distinctions between men and women, nor between heterosexuality and homosexuality. To be biologically male or female would no longer define our social or sexual identities. This does not mean women becoming like men 'for at the same time as we destroy the idea of the generic "Woman", we also destroy the idea of "Man"' (*Questions Féministes* Collective, 1981: 215). It cannot be otherwise since the terms woman/women and man/men are defined in relation to each other and they have no meaning outside this relation. The difference denoted by these terms derives from hierarchy, so that the destruction of sexual hierarchy requires the destruction of difference. This theme was central to the editorial article as a whole, not just Delphy and Plaza's contribution to it, and was fundamental to the journal's theoretical project, defined in opposition to 'neo-femininity' (see Chapter 1). The concept of gender did not, however, feature in this analysis.

Although not widely used in France, the term gender was known to Delphy's circle at this time. Nicole-Claude Mathieu, for example, refers to the sex–gender distinction coined by Stoller (1968) in an article written in 1974 (Mathieu, 1977). It was not, however, widely used. More frequently the distinction between biological males and females on the one hand, and social men and women on the other, is made without recourse to the concept of gender (see, for example, Guillaumin, 1981a, 1981b, 1987). Monique Wittig, reflecting on her article 'The category of sex', written in 1976, comments 'I wanted to show sex as a political category. The word "gender" already used in England and in the United States seemed to me imprecise' (Wittig, 1992: xvi). Wittig therefore uses the term only in the more restricted sense of linguistic gender (Wittig, 1985). Because they questioned sex categories themselves, these feminists saw the sex–gender distinction as essentialist. Delphy attributes the resistance to the concept of gender among other French materialist feminists to the belief that 'it reinforces the idea that "sex" itself is purely natural' (1993a: 5–6).

Although she has always been aware of this problem, Delphy sees the concept of gender more positively. It 'carries within one word both a recognition of the social aspect of the "sexual" dichotomy and the need to treat it as such' (1984: 24). Despite these disagreements on terminology, the broader current of French radical feminism within which Delphy was located was crucially important for her analysis. It provided her with the conceptual tools to pry gender loose from sex and to suggest that the relationship between the two is the reverse of that normally assumed. This was the argument she put in her first explicit discussion of gender in 'Patriarchy, feminism and their intellectuals' (1981b). Here she argues, once again, that we should reject the presuppositions of patriarchal ideology, 'even those which appear . . . to be categories furnished by reality itself, e.g. the categories "women" and "men"' (Delphy, [1981b] 1984: 144). These categories only appear to be natural: they are, in fact, social. They are the result of – and not the foundation for – gender distinctions:

> gender, the respective social position of women and men, is not constructed on the (apparently) natural category of sex (male and female), but rather . . . sex has become a pertinent fact, hence a perceived category, because of the existence of gender. (Delphy, 1984: 144)

This, as she goes on to explain, runs counter to the thinking of many other feminists. Generally anatomical sex is seen as a basic natural division which leads to, or makes possible, social divisions, such as the different tasks allotted to each gender. This in turn is usually thought to create, or permit, gender inequality – the dominance of men over women. In other words, it is commonly thought that the distinction between the sexes logically precedes inequality. Delphy insists, however, that the relationship is the other way round:

> it is *oppression which creates gender* . . . logically the hierarchy of the division of labour is prior to the technical division of labour and created the latter: i.e. created the social roles which we call gender. *Gender in its turn created anatomical sex*, in the sense that the hierarchical division of humanity into two transforms an anatomical difference (which is itself devoid of social implications) into a relevant distinction for social practice. Social practice, and social practice alone, transforms a physical fact (which is itself devoid of meaning, like all physical facts) into a category of thought. (Delphy, 1984: 144; emphasis in original)

She also makes clear, once again, that this position derives from thinking about gender within a class problematic:

> In such a problematic it is not the content of each role which is essential, but the relationship between the roles, between the two groups. This relationship is characterized by hierarchy and it is the latter which explains the content of each role, not the reverse. In this problematic, therefore . . . the key concept is that of *oppression*, which is, or ought to be the key concept of all class problematics. (Delphy, 1984: 145; emphasis in original)

By the early 1980s, then, Delphy had arrived at the position which I outlined at the beginning of this section, the position which continues to inform her recent work. Her materialist conception of gender is not only opposed to biologism, but also to idealism. Gender is not simply a product of ideas about masculinity or femininity, rather it is social practice which makes gender a category of thought. Nor is gender a question of the content of masculine or feminine roles or the value accorded to them: rather the feminine and masculine roles themselves are a product of gender hierarchy – the practices which transform men into the dominant gender and women into subordinates. Implicit in this is an anti-psychologistic perspective. The emphasis on social practice as determinant suggests that gender is not, as psychoanalysts would have it, sustained primarily at the level of our individual psyches.

For Delphy, as we have seen, men and women are *social* groups: 'socially named, socially differentiated, and socially pertinent' (1984: 24). The radical potential of the concept of gender was that it could encapsulate this insight, but at this time only a few feminists fully appreciated the possibilities this opened up. In a paper delivered to a conference at the University of Illinois in 1983, and in the introduction to *Close to Home*, Delphy expressed her disappointment that the concept of gender had not taken off as she had hoped (Delphy, 1984, 1988). While it promised the detachment of the social from the anatomical and biological, this had been only partially achieved. Gender remained attached to sex: 'It is almost never seen on its own, but almost always in composite expressions such as "sex and gender" or sex/gender – the "and" or the slash serving to buttress rather than separate the two' (Delphy, 1984: 24–5). Thus it was widely agreed that the roles and personalities of men and women – the content of gender – were socially defined and varied from society to society, the distinction between the sexes as still assumed to be fixed.

Delphy singles out as an example of this kind of thinking, Gayle Rubin's essay 'The traffic in women: notes on the "political economy" of sex'.[2] This is a recognized feminist classic, generally seen as a major contribution to theories of gender. Rubin conceptualizes the oppression of women in terms of the 'sex/gender system', culturally variable ways of organizing human sexual relations: 'Every society . . . has a sex/gender system – a set of arrangements by which the biological raw material of human sex and procreation is shaped by human, social intervention' (Rubin, 1975: 165). Here we can see clearly the mode of thinking which Delphy is questioning: the 'biological raw material' is taken for granted as creating sexual division in and of itself. As Delphy says:

> Gayle Rubin . . . maintains that in human society sex inevitably gives birth to gender . . . In other words, the fact that humans reproduce sexually and that males and females look different contains within itself not only the capacity but also the *necessity* of a *social* division, albeit the social form varies greatly. The very existence of genders – of different social positions for men and women (or more correctly for females and males) – is thus taken as given and as not requiring explanation. Only the content of these positions and their (eventual, according to Rubin) hierarchy are a matter for investigation. (1984: 25; emphasis in original)

The widespread acceptance of the distinction between natural sex and social gender at this time led Delphy to comment: 'those who, like me, took gender seriously, find themselves today pretty isolated' (1984: 25). Since she wrote those words, others have taken the step of questioning the duality of gender, but this has largely taken place outside a materialist framework (see, for example, Butler, 1990; Davies, 1989). At the same time, however, there has also been a discernible resurgence of feminist perspectives which foreground women's 'difference'. This has prompted Delphy to return to this issue. In recently published articles she begins to develop her conceptualization of gender further while continuing to warn us against the dangers of naturalistic explanations.

Rethinking sex and gender

'Rethinking sex and gender' is the title of an article published in *Women's Studies International Forum* in 1993 in which Delphy offers a more sustained analysis of gender than she had in her previous work. Delphy begins by locating the origins of the idea of gender within an older tradition of work on 'sex roles'. The pioneering work of Margaret Mead (1935) drew on anthropological evidence to demonstrate that traits deemed masculine or feminine varied from one society to another. She thus opened up the possibility of thinking of gender as a cultural construct. Later, between the 1940s and 1950s sociologists began to discuss sex roles in terms of the division of labour in society (Komarovsky, 1950; Michel, 1959, 1960; Myrdal and Klein, 1956). These writers confirmed Mead's view of the arbitrariness of distinctions between the sexes, but they took this further in linking sex roles to work and to differences in status. Hence they introduced the idea that the division between the sexes was both hierarchical and rooted in social structure. Delphy sees this discussion as paving the way for the emergence of the concept of gender. Indeed Ann Oakley's *Sex, Gender and Society*, published in 1972, drew heavily on this previous work in order to refute the claim that social and psychological differences between the sexes are biologically determined. Oakley's book was one of the first works to develop a concept of gender, defined in contradistinction to biological sex. This concept of gender was much wider in scope than the older idea of 'sex roles'. As Delphy comments, the term gender 'covers *all the established differences between men and women*, whether they are individual differences . . . or social roles or cultural representations' (1993a: 3; emphasis in original). What is problematic in Oakley's work, for Delphy, is the lack of emphasis on asymmetry and hierarchy between the genders, and that biological sex is treated as given and invariable. While the former problem has been addressed by subsequent feminist work, the latter has proved more intractable.

In her earlier work Delphy had asserted that the creation of the concept of gender constituted a 'considerable theoretical step forward' in feminist analysis (1984: 24; 1988: 265). Here she elaborates on this, arguing that the concept made three things possible which, as she says, 'does not mean they have happened' (Delphy, 1993a: 3). First, all the differences between the sexes which appear to be social and arbitrary, and which are variable or potentially subject to change, were brought together within one concept. Second, the use of the singular – 'gender' rather than 'genders' – 'allowed the accent to be moved from the two divided parts to the principle of partition itself' (1993a: 3). In other words, the emphasis was on the fact of division between women and men, not simply their separate roles and attributes. Third, the idea of hierarchy became firmly anchored in the concept which should 'have allowed the relationship between the two divided parts to be considered from another angle' (1993a: 3). It is the failure to see gender as the product of hierarchy which, in Delphy's view, has limited the further development of the concept. It is the reasons for this failure which occupy her attention for most of the remainder of this article.

As she says, much research has accumulated to support the conclusion that the content of gender bears no necessary relationship to the biological characteristics of each sex. Yet conceptually little progress has been made:

> We have continued to think of gender in terms of sex: to see it as a social dichotomy determined by a natural dichotomy. We now see gender as the *content* and sex as the *container*. The content may vary . . . but the container is assumed to be invariable because it is part of nature and 'nature does not change'. Moreover, part of the nature of sex is seen to be its *tendency to have a social content*/to vary culturally. (Delphy, 1993a: 3; emphasis in original)

This widely recognized independence of the content of each gender from each sex – of genders from the sexes – should, she says, have prompted us to ask whether gender itself might not be independent of sex. Yet this question has rarely been posed: instead, most writers ask only what sort of social classification sex gives rise to. What is not asked is why sex should give rise to any sort of classification in the first place. Instead it is simply assumed or asserted that sex comes first, both chronologically and logically, but why this should be so is unexplained. Giving precedence to sex in this way effectively means that 'sex causes, or at least explains, gender . . . even if it does not determine the exact forms gender divisions take' (1993a: 4). The theory that sex causes gender can, Delphy argues, arise from only two logical lines of argument.

The first, and more familiar of these, is that the biological characteristics of each sex, usually their procreative functions, are held to necessitate a minimal division of labour. These naturalistic premises are, as Delphy says, to be found in many anthropological accounts, both feminist and non-feminist.[3] Naturalistic arguments fail to give a satisfactory explanation for either this assumed original division of labour or the reasons why it should be extended to areas of activity other than procreation. They therefore fail to explain gender 'other than by propositions which reintroduce upstream one or more elements [they are] supposed to explain downstream' (1993a: 4). In other words, they presuppose part of what they set out to explain. An example she gives elsewhere (Delphy, 1992, 1994) is the argument that childbearing leads to a sexual division of labour. This assumes that the woman who gives birth to a child will necessarily suckle it and will therefore care for all its other needs, that all three functions – childbearing, nursing and childrearing – must all be perfomed by the same person, the 'mother'. This presupposes the prior existence of specific childrearing practices within a specific sexual division of labour. Thus, that which is supposed to be explained 'downstream' – the sexual division of labour – is reintroduced 'upstream' as a precondition for the link made between childbearing and the sexual division of labour. The argument that procreation in and of itself is the basis of gender is therefore flawed.

The second means of arguing that sex gives rise to gender makes no assumptions about a natural division of labour, but sees physical sex as the basis of a system of classification. Biological sex is assumed to have some intrinsic salience which destines it to be used as the basic way in which we categorize human beings. Delphy calls this approach 'cognitivist' because it rests on presumptions about the basis of human cognition, the ways in which we mentally process information:

> It is postulated that human beings have a universal need to establish classifications, independently of and prior to any social organization; and that they also need to establish these classifications on the basis of physical traits, independently of any social practice. But, these two human needs are neither justified nor proven. They are simply asserted. We are not shown *why* sex is more prominent than other physical traits, which are equally distinguishable, but which do not give birth to classifications which are (i) dichotomous and (ii) imply social roles which are not just distinct but hierarchical. (Delphy, 1993a: 4)

Delphy concentrates her critique on a particular variant of this line of argument: that which derives from structuralist and post-structuralist thought. This tradition, from Saussure and Lévi-Strauss through to Derrida is, to many English speakers, what counts as 'French Theory' and has had a major impact on academic feminism (see Chapters 1 and 2). Delphy traces this academic tendency from Saussure's theory of language as a system of differences, through the anthropology of Lévi-Strauss – who claimed that the whole of human society and culture was based on a (presumably pre-social) need to classify the world in terms of sets of binary opposites – through to its recent manifestation in Derrida's conceptualization of 'différance'.[4] Delphy is prepared to accept that we classify the world linguistically, that 'things are known by distinction and hence by differentiation', but argues that these differentiations cannot be reduced to sets of oppositions since they are often multiple. She uses the example of the classification of vegetables: 'Alongside cabbages and carrots, which are not the "opposites" of each other, there are courgettes, melons and potatoes' (Delphy, 1993a: 4). Moreover distinctions, like those between vegetables, are not always hierarchical. We cannot therefore argue from the structure of language to the necessity of dichotomous and hierarchical sexual categories.

A more fundamental problem which Delphy identifies here is that such theories 'fail to distinguish between the differences on which language is based and the differences in social structures' (1993a: 4). Even if human cognition is linguistically ordered, she argues, this cannot account for social hierarchy – this is external to language and cognition. Hence linguistic differentiation cannot account for gender or can do so 'only at the expense of dropping hierarchy as a constitutive element of gender' (Delphy, 1993a: 4–5). This is a crucial point, for it is what distinguishes Delphy's anti-essentialism from that of poststructuralist and postmodernist feminists – an issue I will return to later in this chapter. For now, in order to follow her argument further, we need to note what she has so far established: that the claim that gender is based on sex can only be made from one of two positions – naturalist or cognitivist – and that neither of these is satisfactory. We must therefore, she says, rethink the question of gender's relationship to sex.

If sex cannot be said to cause or give rise to gender, only two other hypotheses are possible. The first is that the correlation between sex and gender is merely coincidental. This is clearly untenable since the correlation is too strong to be due to chance. This leaves one last possibility: that gender *precedes* sex – the position which Delphy has long held. Rather than sex being the basis of gender, 'sex itself simply marks a social division . . . it serves to allow social recognition of those who are dominant and those who are dominated'. Hence 'sex is a sign' and has ' historically acquired a symbolic value' (Delphy, 1993a: 5) because it serves to distinguish two unequal things : men and women. The symbolic significance of sex has, as she says, been recognized by psychoanalysts,[5] but they simply take this for granted as a point of departure without considering why this symbolic differentiation exists.

The sign which differentiates between dominant and dominated categories is related to physical traits, which is why sex is so often seen as natural. Delphy argues, however, that the physical differences we think of as naturally marking out males from females are not as self-evident as we might think: 'The marker is not found in a pure state all ready for use' (Delphy, 1993a: 5). Drawing on the work of Marie-Claude Hurtig and Marie-France Pichevin (1985, 1986), Delphy notes that biologically sex is made up of several indicators, most of which vary in degree. In other words, biologically there is no simple binary division between males and females.[6] In order for sex to become a dichotomous classification, the indicators have to be reduced to just one, and this reduction 'is a social act' (Delphy, 1993a: 5). The generally used indicator is, of course, the presence or absence of a penis.

Now, for all its symbolic significance, the penis is not, in itself, a 'prominent trait'. It is generally thought by cognitivists that this difference *is* a prominent trait, and therefore a suitable vehicle for social classification, because it is linked to functional differences – specifically the ability or inability to bear children – but this is not quite the case. In fact, Delphy argues, the presence or absence of a penis 'does not distinguish tidily between those who can bear children and those who cannot. It distinguishes, in fact, just some of those who cannot'. Many of those without penises cannot bear children, are too young, too old or sterile. It is therefore by no means self-evident that this difference 'exactly cross-checks with the division between potential bearers and non-bearers of children' (Delphy, 1993a: 5).

Questioning these 'facts' conflicts with everyday perceptions of the world. In order to challenge what is so taken for granted, Delphy suggests, we need to pose another question:

> When we compare gender and sex, are we comparing something social with something natural, or are we comparing something social with something which is *also* social (in this case, the way a given society represents 'biology' to itself)? (1993a: 5; emphasis in original)

Delphy suggests that this possibility has rarely been considered. However, in recent years the cultural representation of biological processes has been subjected to considerable scrutiny, challenging ideas about the 'natural', sexed body (see, for example, Jacobus et al., 1990; Laqueur, 1990; Oudshoorn, 1994). This is work Delphy is apparently unfamiliar with – and much of it would have been unavailable to her when she was writing this article. While feminist critiques of science have a long history, the idea that biological sex is a cultural construct is still far from being widely accepted.

As we have seen, those French materialist feminists who rejected the concept of gender did so precisely because it often presupposes a natural distinction between the sexes (gender built on a foundation of biological sex). Delphy continues to defend the concept of gender and argues that 'economising on the concept of gender does not seem to me the best way to progress' (1993a: 6). Because the term 'sex' is already understood to denote and connote something natural, the concept of gender is necessary to 'lay claim to a territory for the social'. Only from this 'strategic location' can we 'challenge the traditional meaning of sex' (1993a: 6).

The issue of the relationship between gender and sex interconnects with that between division and hierarchy. If, Delphy argues, it is accepted that at least some differences are socially constructed this should mean recognizing that hierarchy forms the basis for this difference. This has political implications, since it means that if we could do away with hierarchy we would also do away with differences. What troubles Delphy is the reluctance of many feminists to accept this conclusion. While all feminists share the goal of abolishing the hierarchy through which men dominate women, many seem to want to keep some aspects of the distinctiveness of each gender: 'They want to abolish the contents, but not the container . . . Very few indeed are happy to contemplate there being simply anatomical sex differences which are not given any social significance or symbolic value' (Delphy, 1993a: 6). Delphy sees this as characteristic not only of those who see difference as prior to hierarchy, but also those who accept that difference is socially constructed as the product of hierarchy. It is evident, for example, in the concern of many feminists to preserve feminine values, despite the widespread recognition that values are social constructs. She identifies two variants of this position. One wishes to keep feminine values as the preserve of women, the other wants to distribute masculine and feminine values among both women and men. In both cases, she argues, there is an implicit contradiction of the problematic of gender. On the one hand, the desire to retain gender categories indicates that gender is not, after all, thought of as a social classification. On the other there is a conceptualization of values in which all human potential is assumed to already be represented within our culture, but divided up between men and women. Hence masculine plus feminine subcultures (and by implication culture itself) are seen as independent of the hierarchical society within which they are produced. This, as Delphy says, 'is contrary to everything we know about the relationship between social structure and culture' (1993a: 7). The values which exist within a given society will be appropriate to its social structure hence a hierarchical society will give rise to hierarchically arranged values. Masculinity and femininity, along with the values associated with them, do not represent a division of pre-existing traits and values, nor do they together represent the sum total of human potential:

> (M)asculinity and femininity are the cultural creations of a society based on gender hierarchy . . . This means not only that they are linked together in a relationship of complementarity and opposition, but also that this structure determines the *content of each of these categories* and not just their relationship. It may be that together they cover the totality of human traits *which exist today*, but we cannot presume that even together they cover the whole of human potentialities . . . changing the respective statuses of the groups would lead to neither an alignment of all individuals on a single model, nor a happy hybrid between the two models. (Delphy, 1993a: 7)

We cannot, Delphy argues, assume that the feminine or masculine models exist in themselves, independent of social structure, nor can we assume that they would exist in any future society with a different social structure. To think in this way presupposes an 'untenable, static view of culture' and assumes 'the invariability of a universal human subject' – a view of human nature now well and truly invalidated by all that is known about the historical and social construction of subjectivity (Delphy, 1993a: 7). There is, therefore, no foundation for the often expressed fear that equality with men would mean becoming like men. If we think within a gender framework, then men are what they are because they are members of a dominant group: if they no longer had another group – women – to dominate they would no longer be the same: 'If women were the equals of men, men would no longer equal themselves. Why then should women resemble what men have ceased to be?' (Delphy, 1993a: 8). Nor can we envisage a future egalitarian society as based on some combination of current masculine and feminine values, because these values 'were created in and by hierarchy'. So how, Delphy asks, 'could they survive the end of hierarchy?' (1993a: 8).

For Delphy, the naturalistic conceptualization of values as existing independently of the hierarchical society within which they were constructed is part of a wider configuration of ideas. This includes 'a double confusion of anatomical sex with sexuality, and sexuality with procreation'. A related, deep cultural theme is that each individual is incomplete insofar as she or he is sexed, but that somehow we complement each other. The emblem of this complementarity is 'the image of heterosexual intercourse, and this gives it a social meaning and an emotional charge which is explicable only by its symbolic value' (1993a: 8). Heterosexuality is represented as 'fitting together', which turns on a belief in the 'naturalness' of intimate bonds between men and women. These sets of beliefs have, Delphy says, a 'mystical and non-rational character': they constitute a 'cosmogony'. She signposts this as something which requires further investigation, particularly the way in which this cosmogony informs much scientific, including feminist, research.[7] In the context of this article, the main point is that this way of thinking prevents us from realizing the radical potential of the concept of gender: 'perhaps we shall only really be able to think about gender on the day when we can imagine non-gender' (Delphy, 1993a: 9).

The politics of difference

The desire to preserve certain traditional feminine values is perhaps understandable in a society which has always devalued the feminine, and might seem to pose a challenge to the masculine values which govern a patriarchal society. For materialist feminists, and other radical feminists who take an anti-essentialist stance, this desire is dangerous because it reinforces the very gender divisions which we should, as feminists, be seeking to undermine. Delphy is not alone in being troubled by this tendency – it has also been heavily criticized, for example, by Andrea Dworkin (1978) and by Monique Wittig (1981, 1992). Both of these writers share Delphy's concern that it all too easily leads us back to a celebration of a 'natural' femininity and even to a position where some form of moral or biological superiority is claimed for women. Despite criticism, the idea of women's specificity continues to inform aspects of feminist theory and politics, in particular the demand for specific rights for women *as* women.

One particular variant of this which has recently come to the fore is what Delphy calls the 'maternal demand' (1992, 1994). She does not mean by this a single, clearly articulated political demand, but rather a general tendency, in a range of feminist writings and campaigns, to ground claims to women's rights in biological maternity. Within this tendency rights are claimed and liberation sought on the grounds of women's specificity, and this specificity is based upon women's reproductive function. In demanding what Delphy calls 'exorbitant' rights as mothers, rights not accorded to everyone, other rights are implicitly renounced. Such demands run counter to feminists' demands for common treatment based on universalistic premises, on membership of the human species. It is not only the reassertion of difference which Delphy finds disquieting here, but also the assumptions which are made about children, the assertion of women's 'ownership' of them (see Chapter 3) on the basis of assumed natural ties between mothers and children (Delphy, 1991a, 1992, 1993b, 1994).

Delphy explores these issues in terms of feminist writings on reproductive technology and human evolution, as well as in forms of feminism premised on ideas about 'maternal values' (Delphy,

1992, 1994). In all these areas Delphy detects essentialist assumptions about the 'naturalness' of the mother–child tie, which is identified as the only biological link that matters and as the 'natural' basis of human kinship. Feminists who are critical of the assumed normality of patrilineal descent, descent through the male line, often end up asserting their own version of 'naturalness': descent through the female line. Hence they fail to recognize that 'whatever form descent may take, it is *always* a social convention' (Delphy, 1992: 15; emphasis in original). What is at stake here is a claim to some form of natural, exclusive relation between mothers and children and hence mothers' natural rights to children.

This is the thinking behind forms of feminist theory which locate women's specificity in maternal values. Delphy identifies writers, such as Gilligan (1982) and Ruddick (1980), who assert that gender differences are socially constructed but still assume that similar values are somehow shared by all women by virtue of biological maternity. Cultural diversity and historical change are therefore ignored. What are defined as universal 'feminine values' are, in fact, 'a collection of very specific values, which correspond more or less to those of western housewives of the last half century' (1992: 18). These 'maternal values' are seen as the positive aspect of femininity, as worthy of preservation by feminists. Hence the patriarchal identification of women with motherhood is reinstated in feminist guise. Where, Delphy asks, does this leave childless women? Often it leaves them having to justify their childlessness to other feminists lest they be suspected of being insufficiently altruistic, nurturant or peace-loving (Delphy, 1994: 195).

The belief in a 'natural' or even 'sacred' bond between mother and child, then, carries with it the notion that women embody maternal values. This in turn often justifies the claim that women are self-evidently better parents than men. It is in these terms that mothers' rights are asserted in opposition to fathers' rights:

> mothers are seen not in terms of what they have in common with fathers, in terms of their being adults in relation to children, but solely in opposition to and in terms of their differences from fathers, from men. Mothers are everything men are not and vice-versa. Men are competitive, women are co-operative; men are violent, women are pacific; men are incestuous, women are not – or hardly at all; men are egoistic, women are altruistic. (Delphy, 1994: 196)

Children's dependence on adults, and specifically parents, is thus taken for granted. The only protection against the bad parent (the father) is assumed to be the good parent (the mother). Why children should be so dependent on their parents is not questioned – it is accepted as natural. The power and rights that adults have over children are justified in terms of children's specificity, just as the rights women as mothers claim over them are defined in terms of feminine specificity. The logical absurdities of this, as Delphy says, go unquestioned. Hence we lump children together in their supposed 'specificity' – their incapacity to look after themselves – forgetting the range of ages and competencies that childhood encompasses and forgetting, too, that children's dependence is something we encourage and foster. In many respects this focus on their specificity denies their common humanity with adults, just as women's rights to full human status have historically been denied (Delphy, 1993b, 1994). The assertion of women's specificity similarly lumps all women together – this time on the basis of an assumed shared capacity to be maternal. It is clear that these 'differences' are not merely there to be recognized, but are socially constructed.

Here, then, Delphy has widened the scope of her analysis of gender to draw parallels between the position of women and the position of children. Her opposition to essentialism leads her to question not only the distinction between males and females, but also that between children and adults. In so doing she reminds us that '*nothing* is natural in human society' (Delphy, 1994: 196; emphasis in original).

Critiques and developments

Some of the work dealt with in this chapter, in particular that on maternal values, is too recent to have given rise to published critiques and may yet prove highly controversial.[8] Her perspective on gender, however, has long been established and has not changed substantially since the early 1980s. This aspect of her work has received remarkably little critical attention, which is perhaps surprising given that it is so interconnected with her thinking on women and men as classes. She herself has said that when she first suggested that gender creates sex (makes it socially significant), it was not understood.[9] The idea that the very existence of gender categories should be challenged was then very new, and it is indeed possible that many feminists, even within academia, would have found it alien or incomprehensible.

Although it remains controversial, such radical anti-essentialism has now become more academically fashionable – particularly among poststructuralists and postmodernists. These theorists frequently claim to take their inspiration from 'French feminism', but this generally excludes materialist feminists – with the notable exception of Monique Wittig, whose work has been considered in some depth by both Diana Fuss (1989) and Judith Butler (1990). As a consequence, Wittig's writings on sex differences, which share Delphy's basic premises, have become rather better known. This raises the question of why Wittig has been taken up within these debates on gender while Delphy has largely been ignored. In part this may derive from the wider availability of Wittig's work in the United States – due to its publication in *Feminist Issues* , which ceased to print Delphy's work after the split within the *Questions Féministes* collective in 1980[10] – and the fact that Wittig is herself based in the USA. Wittig also deals extensively with questions of language and with the discursive construction of sexual categories, which has considerable appeal to postmodernist philosophers and literary theorists. One major reason for the attention given to Wittig is her perspective on lesbianism, which is of particular interest to those who, like Fuss and Butler, are concerned with the interconnections between gender and sexuality. Reading Wittig in isolation from other materialist feminists, however, leads to interpretations of her work which undermine its materialist foundations.

It is worth considering Wittig's work in its own right, since it represents a development of the perspective on sexual divisions which emerged among the *Questions Féministes* collective in the late 1970s. It should be remembered that at that time, prior to the rift between them, Delphy and Wittig were working closely together – so the convergence of their ideas is hardly surprising. There are, however, important differences between them. Wittig shares Delphy's view, that there are no natural sex categories pre-existing hierarchy: 'It is oppression that creates sex and not the contrary' (Wittig, 1992: 2). Like Delphy, she sees sexual divisions as a product of a class relationship:

> [T]he category 'woman' as well as the category 'man' are political and economic categories, not eternal ones . . . Once the class 'men' disappears, 'women' as a class will disappear as well, for there are no slaves without masters. (Wittig, 1992: 15)

Wittig places particular emphasis on heterosexuality as the locus of women's oppression: 'The category of sex is the political category that founds society as heterosexual' (1992: 5). Where Wittig differs radically from Delphy is in her assertion that lesbians, fugitives from the heterosexual contract, escape from the category 'women', are not women (1980, 1981). While it is this aspect of her work which has attracted the attention of American theorists of gender, both Fuss (1989) and Butler (1990) are critical of the essentialism implied by treating lesbianism as lying outside the cultural construction and regulation of gender and sexuality. This is an argument with which Delphy would concur, given that she sees heterosexuality and homosexuality as culturally constructed in the same way as gender.

Butler's (1990) radical deconstruction of gender owes a great deal to materialist feminism, but is not itself materialist. She does not read Wittig in the context of the thinkers whom Wittig herself (1992: xiv) names as her chief political influences, such as Mathieu, Delphy and Guillaumin, but in conjunction with Foucault, Lacan, Derrida, Kristeva and Irigaray. Although she is aware of differences between materialist and other French feminisms, her postmodernist reading of Wittig filters out much which is fundamental to materialism. In the first place Butler oversexualizes Wittig's conceptualization of heterosexuality. According to Butler, Wittig sees the binary sexual divide as 'serving the reproductive aims of a system of compulsory heterosexuality' (Butler, 1990: 19), and as restricting 'the production of identities along the axis of heterosexual desire' (1990: 26). Wittig does place great emphasis on women's sexual servicing of men, but she also makes it clear that the heterosexual contract involves a good deal more than coitus and reproduction:

> The category of sex is the product of a heterosexual society in which men appropriate for themselves the reproduction and production of women and also their physical persons by means of . . . the marriage contract. (1992: 6)

This contract 'assigns the woman certain obligations, including unpaid work' (Wittig, 1992: 7). She goes on to argue that it determines control of a woman's children and where she should live, makes her dependent on her husband, subject to his authority, and denies her the full protection of the law if he assaults her. Elsewhere she explains that what lesbians escape from is a relation 'which implies personal and physical obligation as well as economic obligation' ([1981] 1992: 20). All this echoes Delphy's analysis of the class relation between men and women (see Chapters 3 and 4) and Guillaumin's work on sexual difference and on the private and collective appropriation of women's labour (Guillaumin, 1981a, 1981b, 1987). Butler, however, ignores these material social relations underpinning the category of sex.

Butler does appear to understand that 'materialism takes social institutions and practices . . . as the basis of critical analysis' (1990:125), but she fails to recognize that, for materialists, this implies a system of structural inequalities. Because Wittig's references to such structural inequalities are absent from Butler's summary of her work, we are left with the impression of sexual difference as oppressive, yet not clearly hierarchical: 'Wittig understands "sex" to be discursively produced and circulated by a system of significations oppressive to women, gays and lesbians' (Butler, 1990: 113). Wittig's work is thus shaped to fit Butler's own contention that gender is a 'regulatory fiction' to which both women and men are subject, but which is sustained – and can be subverted – through performance.[11] Butler's work is an example of what Delphy means when she says, in 'Rethinking sex and gender' (1993a), that perspectives deriving from Derrida's 'cognitive' approach can account for gender only at the expense of ignoring hierarchy. Because for Butler gender has no material basis, her anti-essentialism leads to the conclusion that women do not exist except as a discursive construct. For Delphy and Wittig, however, women exist as a political category, as a class, because of patriarchy. There may be no natural basis for the category 'women', but it is a material, social reality (see Jackson, 1992b).

The disjunction between materialist and postmodernist views of gender is addressed by Michèle Barrett in her comment on Delphy's contribution to a conference at the University of Chicago (Barrett, 1988; Delphy, 1988). She suggests that feminist perspectives on the social constitution of gender can be placed on a continuum between two 'extreme positions':

> At one end (and I would locate Christine here) is a theory which sees gender as, in a sense, a Durkheimian social fact.[12] What we are studying when we look at the acquisition of gender is the acquisition of a social identity that is already there. At the opposite pole is the theoretical view that there is no such fixed category already there but, rather, that the meaning of gender – the meaning of femininity and masculinity – is constructed anew in every encounter. (Barrett, 1988: 268)

If Delphy's work is located at one end of the continuum, then it would be fair to place Butler at the other end, which Barrett associates with discourse theory.[13] Barrett is critical of both views, seeing Delphy's 'Durkheimian' position as unable to account for change in the meaning of gender, while discourse theory cannot explain the persistence of gender. This latter criticism is one which materialists would endorse, but Barrett's portrayal of Delphy's position is not entirely accurate. Delphy certainly does not see femininity and masculinity as fixed and unchanging: that the content of gender categories varies from one society to another and changes over time is fundamental to her critique of naturalism. Yet Barrett is, in part, correct in saying that Delphy's critique treats gender as a 'social identity which is already there', because Delphy does consider that gender divisions are fully social and therefore exist prior to individuals. She does indeed invoke Durkheim in calling gender a social fact which therefore requires a social explanation (Delphy, 1988: 265). Another feature of social facts, according to Durkheim, is that they are external to any given member of society and impose constraints upon us. This latter is little different from Marx's assertion that as human individuals we enter into social and economic relations which are independent of our will (Marx in McLellan, 1977: 389). It amounts to saying that there is such a thing as social structure over which we, as individuals, have little or no control. Gender is, for Delphy, rooted in social structure – but this does not mean that nothing changes.

One problem with Barrett's commentary on Delphy is that she fails to distinguish between the content of gender – what we know as masculinity and femininity – and the container, the fact of gender division itself. This distinction *is* made by Delphy in the conference paper Barrett is commenting on, and it makes a difference. Ideas about masculinity and femininity, the roles and identities men and women can take on, can and do change – and have done so even in the past few decades under the impact of feminism. On the other hand, the gender divide itself, the hierarchical division between the sexes, is much less amenable to change and remains an intractable fact of social life. There are certainly more questions which could be raised here about the relationship between the 'content' and 'container', about how 'men' and 'women' are constituted as such in different societies and in different epochs. Some materialist feminists have begun to look at this (Mathieu, 1980; Tabet, 1982), but there is, as Delphy herself says (1984, 1988, 1993a), still a great deal more work to be done on this and other aspects of gender. A further problem here, one which Barrett does not raise, is that Delphy's focus on patriarchal relations per se, rather than their interrelationship with other systems of dominance and subordination, means that she has little to say about the intersections between gender and other social divisions – such as racial hierarchies – or the resultant differences among women.

There is another issue implied by Barrett here when she talks of the 'acquisition of gender' – the relationship between the structural hierarchy of gender and the ways in which we come to inhabit it, in other words the problem of subjectivity. Much feminist writing about gender does focus on subjectivity – on how we acquire feminine or masculine identities and how gender shapes our thoughts and desires. Delphy has never made subjectivity as such a central element of her work, but this does not mean she considers it unimportant. In 'For a materialist feminism', she made it clear that subjectivity could and should be studied from a materialist perspective and thereby reclaimed from psychologism. Here she suggests that subjectivity should be seen 'as one of the expressions, if not one of the mechanisms, of social organization' (Delphy, 1984:

217), but that – unfortunately – the links are usually made in the opposite direction. Hence social practices are thought of as deriving from subjectivity: 'psychologism [has] not even limited itself to the study of subjectivity, but has grabbed the study of interaction, of groups, and even of institutions' (Delphy, 1984: 217). She implies that a materialist perspective should treat subjectivity as embedded in social practice, as shaped by material social relations. Delphy does not attempt to construct such a theory, but nor have other feminists. Despite the widespread acceptance of Beauvoir's dictum that 'one is not born, but becomes, a woman', the process by which this happens is still remarkably undertheorized outside psychoanalysis. It remains a largely uncharted area for materialist feminism.

It is clear, then, that Delphy wishes to reclaim the study of gender from both psychologism and biologism. This is by no means uncontroversial. As well as those feminists committed to psychoanalytic explanations, there are those who do not think we should ignore biology. One variant of this argument is raised by Barrett. While she agrees in principle with Delphy's rejection of naturalistic arguments, she feels that feminists should not ignore or dismiss them, since they are so well entrenched in popular thinking on gender (Barrett, 1988). We cannot therefore afford the luxury of 'saying that biological . . . arguments should not be addressed by feminists' (1988: 269). But is this what Delphy is saying? In the conference paper these remarks are addressed to, she expresses her exasperation at having to deal with each new variant of biological determinism. She is critical of those feminists who think that 'we must take account of biology', asking why we should do so (1988: 264). My reading of this is that Delphy is querying arguments which say we should 'take account of biology' in the sense of accepting that gender has a biological component, not that she is turning her back on attempts to refute biology. Indeed she has, throughout her work, countered the logic of biological determinism. She certainly asks why the question of the biological basis of gender continues to be posed, but she is not unaware of the continued popularity of biologistic arguments. Barrett calls for a more serious engagement with, and refutations of, pseudo-scientific arguments. Delphy's more recent work, I would suggest, begins to answer this call.

Diana Fuss also cites Delphy's questioning of the idea that 'we mustn't ignore biology' (Delphy, 1984: 23; Fuss, 1989: 51) and, like Barrett, reads this as meaning that we should simply ignore biology. The source on this occasion is the introduction to *Close to Home*. In the context of this volume no one could – or should – accuse Delphy of not giving biological arguments 'serious theoretical attention' (Fuss, 1989: 51).[14] She does, however, refuse to give them any credence. Fuss has some more specific problems with Wittig and Delphy: it worries her that they do not treat the body as material and that they fail to theorize the relationship between anatomical females and social women. What is missing from Wittig's work – and by implication from Delphy's – is, she says, 'a materialist analysis of the body *as* matter' (Fuss, 1989: 50; emphasis in original). This implies that materialists should treat the body as matter and confuses philosophical materialism with marxist materialism (see Chapter 2). Whereas the former does treat the body as a material fact, French materialist feminism, taking its cue from marxism, prioritizes social relations. Hence the physical or anatomical bodies of women and men are not what matters, but rather the social meanings they acquire – meanings which in turn derive from the hierarchical division of society by gender. A similar misunderstanding underlies Butler's claim that 'Wittig is a classic idealist for whom nature is understood as a mental representation' (1990: 125). What she misses here is that gender is not merely 'an "idea" generated and sustained for purposes of hierarchical control' (Butler, 1990: 125). It is founded on material social relations and social practices: the exploitation of women as a class.

Materialist feminists do not simply shut their eyes to natural facts. They do not, as Fuss implies, refuse to deal with the physical facts of bodily existence. For example, in 'Proto-feminism and antifeminism' (reprinted in *Close to Home)* Delphy offers a three page discussion of menstruation in order to demonstrate that it is never simply a natural process:

> A particular culture not only imposes a meaning on an event which, being physical, is in and of itself bereft of meaning. Society (culture) also imposes a material form through which the event is lived, or rather is moulded in a constraining way . . . You do not have 'a' period, the

> same in all situations and all countries. You have *your* period, different in each culture and subculture. ([1976a] 1984: 194; emphasis in original)

Delphy has never claimed that there are no biological differences between the sexes. On the very page of *Close to Home* from which Fuss quotes she says: 'No one is denying the anatomical differences between male and female humans or their different parts in producing babies' (Delphy, 1984: 23). What she does deny, and has denied consistently from her earliest work to her most recent is that these differences are socially significant in themselves. When Fuss suggests that we might learn more about the social construction of gender by 'interrogating the relations between female and woman, woman and women' (1989: 52) she is posing, from a materialist point of view, the wrong question. What we need to ask instead is what produces and sustains the social division which makes biological femaleness socially meaningful. Delphy's argument, as I hope I have made clear in this chapter, is that we cannot assume that pre-given biological categories provide a foundation for gender: sex categories are themselves socially constructed, they are a product of gender hierarchy.

Notes

1. There is another perspective within which the categories 'women' and 'men' themselves are seen as socially constructed: the phenomenological and ethnomethodological tradition within sociology. Feminists influenced by this perspective were also making this point long before poststructuralism and postmodernism became fashionable. See, for example, the work of Liz Stanley and Sue Wise (1983), which drew on this tradition. For more recent appraisals of this approach see the debate on feminism and ethnomethodology in the journal *Gender and Society*, 6 (2) 1992.

2. Delphy does not offer a summary or exposition of Rubin's work – possibly because it was so widely known and cited at the time. For the benefit of those unfamiliar with Rubin's argument, I have provided slightly more detail and quoted from her article in order to clarify the points which Delphy critiques.

3 There are, she notes in passing, a few exceptions to this, such as the work of Nicole-Claude Mathieu (1991) and Paola Tabet (1982) – both of whom are materialist feminists.

4. It should be noted here that considerable changes have taken place within this theoretical tradition. The early structuralist position represented by Lévi-Strauss assumed a relatively stable set of linguistic and cultural structures, whereas

Derrida's poststructuralism emphasizes the ways in which meanings constantly shift, so that there is no final guarantor of meaning. Delphy's critique, however, is addressed to the common assumptions underpinning this form of theory, not its many variants. The most accessible account of poststructuralism and its potential relevance to feminism is Chris Weedon's (1987) – but beware of her gross misrepresentation of radical feminism.

5. This is particularly true of the French school of psychoanalysis deriving from the work of Jacques Lacan and his followers.

6. The work of Hurtig and Pichevin is published only in French. For similar arguments in English, see Anne Fausto-Sterling (1989, 1992).

7. In personal correspondence she has expressed a desire to investigate this further, but has not yet done so.

8. Delphy's position on motherhood conflicts with that of many other radical feminists working around such issues as reproductive technology. For example, she is sceptical of apocalyptic visions of femicide and women replaced by artificial wombs. In the first place, she argues we are technologically a long way from this being feasible. In the second, women's capacity to bear children is far from being the only use which patriarchy has for us – the work women do for men is far more important (see Chapter 3). Feminists' willingness to give such priority to reproduction, she says, takes patriarchal ideology at face value – 'women are only good for having babies' (Delphy, 1994: 189).

9. Personal correspondence.

10. See Chapter 1.

11. A materialist feminist analysis by no means excludes the idea of gender as performance: both Guillaumin (1987) and Wittig (1982) point to the ways in which sexual difference is sustained through codes of conduct, dress and demeanour. The point, however, is that this is symptomatic of gender hierarchy and not an independent means by which gender is maintained. The performance is therefore, in a sense, coerced: women 'must wear their yellow star, their constant smile, day and night' (Wittig, [1982] 1992: 7).

12. Durkheim was a French sociologist writing in the late nineteenth and early twentieth centuries and one of the acknowledged founders of modern sociology. He developed the concept of the 'social fact' in *The Rules of the Sociological Method* (1982).

13. Butler's *Gender Trouble* was published several years after these comments were made, but nonetheless serves as a good example of Barrett's point.

14. Delphy deals explicitly with biological arguments in two articles reprinted in *Close to Home*: 'Patriarchy, feminism and their intellectuals' and 'Proto-feminism and anti-feminism'.

6

Conclusion: Feminist Knowledge and Feminist Politics

I began this book by describing Delphy as both a theorist and an activist. She would see these two aspects of her life as intimately interconnected, since she regards feminist theory and activism as indispensable to each other. For Delphy feminist theory is not, and should not be, something abstract and distant from grass-roots activism – it has no purpose unless it furthers women's political struggle. Conversely, the possibility of feminist theory derives from the existence of the women's movement. Feminist knowledge seeks to explain women's oppression and therefore presupposes a collective understanding of our situation *as* one of oppression (Delphy, 1975, 1980b, 1981a, 1981b). Without such an understanding, deriving from the women's movement, her own materialist analysis of women's subordination could never have been developed, for 'as long as an area of experience stays outside the class struggle, it remains out of reach of materialism' (Delphy, 1984: 217).

Delphy maintains that feminist knowledge should serve the movement which made it possible. Her materialism is therefore a political stance as well as a theoretical one. Delphy (1975, 1981b) sees in materialism the only perspective which is both designed to explain oppression and which treats oppression as fully social in origin (see Chapter 2). This is why, although she never claims to have established a total theory of women's subordination, she nonetheless believes that a materialist analysis is fundamental to women's liberation. Such an analysis implies particular priorities for the feminist movement. First, it presupposes that women's oppression is important in its own right and distinct from other oppressions, thus establishing the need for an autonomous women's movement. Second, if women's oppression is material and social, this implies that the primary aim of the women's movement is to change the institutional structures and social practices which maintain this oppression, rather than concentrating primarily on its ideological or psychological components. The latter factors are not unimportant to Delphy, since political action requires a political consciousness and challenging existing social structures means combating the patriarchal ideologies which help sustain them. Changes in consciousness or ideology, however, are not ends in themselves, but means to an end: hence Delphy's constant vigilance against idealism and psychologism. When Delphy engages in polemic against those who espouse these positions, she is not engaged in a purely academic debate or simply seeking to score points against theoretical rivals. Rather, she seeks to warn against positions which she feels will undermine the political aims of the feminist movement.

Similarly, her persistent opposition to naturalistic accounts of relations between men and women, her insistence that gender divisions and family structures have no natural foundations, is fundamental to her vision of feminism's goals. Feminist struggle aims to change the conditions which produce women's subordination. If those conditions were natural it would be futile to try to change them; conversely trying to change them implies that they are social in origin.

> People do not revolt against what is natural, therefore inevitable; or inevitable, therefore natural. Since what is resistible is not inevitable; what is not inevitable could be otherwise – it is arbitrary therefore social. The logical and necessary implication of women's revolt, like all

> revolts, is that the situation can be changed. Belief in the possibility of change implies belief in the social origins of the situation. (Delphy, 1984: 211)

The idea that relations between the sexes are natural is therefore anti-feminist. If women believe this, they will accept their lot; if men believe it, they will not question their dominance. Hence naturalism is an ideology which serves to justify women's subordination, to legitimize it in the eyes of both oppressor and oppressed. This is why Delphy finds it so necessary to root out instances of essentialist thinking wherever she finds them: including in the work of other feminists.

As well as producing knowledge which furthers women's struggle, Delphy also feels that it is important that we record the history of that struggle. This in itself makes an important contribution to both feminist scholarship and the women's movement. If we as feminists do not tell our own history, she argues, it will vanish and 'the few centimetres snatched from our oppressors through our struggle' will be represented as a result of the inevitable march of progress (Delphy, [1980a] 1987b: 34). We know from the demise of first wave feminism after the vote was won that 'our movements are mortal' (Delphy, 1987b: 39). She therefore believes that we have a historical responsibility to future generations of women to ensure that our struggles and our movement do not vanish from the record, so that they do not have to reinvent feminism from scratch. History is not simply a narrative about the past: particular representations of that past can serve specific interests. Hence history is itself the site of struggle. This is why Delphy has felt it necessary to counteract misrepresentations of MLF, both those originating within France, from *Psych et Po*'s leader, Antionette Fouque, and those arising from the Anglo-American version of 'French feminism' (Delphy, 1980a, 1991b, 1995).

Feminist knowledge and women's studies

Delphy defines feminist knowledge as knowledge which takes women's oppression as its starting point, which seeks to explain it and which serves our political interests (1975, 1981a, 1981b). In so doing she anticipated issues which have become central to feminist scholarship. Her view of feminist knowledge poses a considerable challenge to mainstream academia, particularly to the ideals of politically disinterested objectivity on which traditional social science has been founded. Many feminists have now taken up this challenge, and the issue of what counts as feminist knowledge, of how specifically feminist methodologies and epistemologies differ from more traditional approaches, has become the subject of considerable debate (see, for example, Harding, 1987; Maynard and Purvis, 1994; Smith, 1988; Stanley and Wise, 1983, 1993). At the same time, the incorporation of feminism and women's studies in the academy raises issues about the relationship between academic feminists and the wider women's movement. Delphy's insistence on the necessary interrelationship between feminist theory and feminist politics is obviously relevant to both of these concerns.

When Delphy first formulated her ideas on feminist knowledge in 'For a materialist feminism' (1975), feminist activism was at a high point while women's studies was still in its infancy. At the time she was addressing an activist audience as much as an academic one. Her ideas may well be read differently now, given that women's studies has become more established while the women's movement has become more fragmented. This is not to say that feminist activism, or the link between theory and politics, have ceased to be important. The growth of women's studies is itself a product of feminist struggle both within and outside academic institutions. Although its presence in the academy can serve to distance feminist theory from the politics in which it was once rooted, it has created new possibilities for feminist scholarship and new audiences for feminist ideas. Feminism has also had an impact on mainstream academic theory and research, notably within Delphy's own discipline of sociology (see Maynard, 1990). Hence many feminists might feel that Delphy's criticisms of sociology are no longer of any salience. We should not forget, however, that any such changes in the wider context of academic work are the product of feminists' persistent attacks on the patriarchal biases which Delphy identifies. Moreover, we cannot afford to be complacent about feminism's acceptability in the academy, and it is worth noting that this may be greater in many Western countries than it is in Delphy's native France (see Armengaud et al., 1995).

I will return to the theme of feminism's impact on sociology, but first I want to say more about Delphy's critique of traditional, pre-feminist social science. Delphy's work exemplifies what is fundamental to the production of feminist knowledge – its challenge to the androcentric bias of mainstream academic theory and research. Although her training as a sociologist has certainly influenced her theory, Delphy is also very critical of her own discipline. In her work on the family and on class she has exposed the patriarchal thinking underlying much sociological work. There are aspects of sociology which are conducive to a feminist analysis, particularly the emphasis on the social origin of social phenomena, but Delphy detects a hidden naturalism underlying many so-called sociological approaches to gender divisions. An example of this which Delphy has consistently challenged is that sociologists have accepted the division of labour and inequality within families as given and have thus treated these phenomena as if they lie outside the realm of the social. She is not alone in mounting such critiques. Many feminist scholars have questioned what counts as 'objective' knowledge, demonstrating that much of social science is fundamentally flawed by its androcentrism. Social scientific knowledge has frequently excluded women, has claimed to produce knowledge about society as a whole which is in effect knowledge only about men produced from a masculine standpoint. Feminists have also become increasingly aware that it is not sufficient to simply add women into existing bodies of knowledge, to make them visible, but that taking account of women's oppression means challenging the basis of mainstream academic knowledge at a far more fundamental level (see, for example, Harding, 1987; Smith, 1988; Stanley and Wise, 1983, 1993).

Delphy (1975, 1981a) argues that understanding women's situation as one of oppression radically challenges the basic premises of social science, particularly its denial of women's oppression: 'A feminist – or proletarian – science aims at explaining oppression' (Delphy, [1975] 1984: 212), and to do so has to start with oppression and create a theory of history as the domination of one group by another. It is a basic premise of materialism that science or knowledge can never be absolutely objective in that it is always produced from within a particular social location. Where others may try to pass off 'science' as universal 'truth', materialists recognize that knowledge is a human, social construct and that it therefore serves the interests of particular social groups. Knowledge which claims objectivity for itself is usually knowledge which supports the status quo. Delphy argues that a feminist interpretation of history is therefore a materialist one in that intellectual production is seen as the result of social relationships, and the latter are seen as relationships of domination.

Since knowledge is a social product, the particular organization of knowledge within which we work presupposes particular assumptions about human nature and the nature of the social. This is particularly so of the current ordering of academic disciplines. Delphy sees the division of knowledge into disciplines and the content of each discipline as 'an effect and a tool of ideology' ([1975] 1984: 213) and as anti-materialist. This division of knowledge assumes that different aspects or levels of social life are distinct from each other and should be studied separately using different methods. The example Delphy gives is marriage. If we take the usual division of labour between the disciplines we might find the relations between husbands and wives being studied in different ways by different social scientists, with psychologists studying their sexual relations, sociologists studying marriage as a social relationship and economists studying the economics of marriage. What we end up with is a very partial account of marriage which prevents us from understanding the interrelationship between these various aspects of it. Even if, in an effort at interdisciplinarity, we bring these various findings together we end up with 'an uninteresting mosaic' rather than a coherent view of the whole. The effect is 'the rendering unintelligible of human experience' (Delphy, 1984: 213).

Rejecting this cutting up of knowledge into disciplines does not mean refusing to recognize that different levels of experience exist; rather it entails a refusal to see any level of experience in isolation and, in particular, an emphasis on the social and political relevance of all aspects of experience. For example, this materialist feminist approach challenges psychoanalysis, not because it 'suggests the existence of a purely subjective level, but because it imputes to this level a content independent of social relationships' (Delphy, 1984: 215). This insistence on the pre-eminence of the social, Delphy insists, is not the result of a sociological chauvinism, but of a theoretical position opposed to the specialisms of the disciplines. It is not simply about asserting the importance of the social, but of recognizing that the social is political.

Delphy argues that we cannot hope to understand women's oppression within the framework of existing disciplines, but must question their epistemological foundations. Each discipline, Delphy explains, constructs its own objects, delimits its own field of study and constructs knowledge according to its own premises. Since these premises 'do not posit men/women relationships as relationships of oppression [they] posit them, by commission or omission, as something else' (Delphy, 1984: 214). Hence although social scientists have studied areas of social life and subjective experience in which women are oppressed, this oppression is made to disappear. As a field of knowledge which starts from the oppression of women, women's studies cannot be content with simply questioning specific findings from other disciplines. It must challenge every aspect of those disciplines' concepts and methods, how particular results were obtained and interpreted and also how a particular object of study was constituted. Even the most technical and neutral concepts should be subject to scrutiny since they are unlikely to be merely technical and neutral. An example might be the sociological concept of 'class' which appears to describe an objectively existing social phenomenon, but which has had the effect of defining sexual inequality, and indeed women themselves, out of existence (see Chapter 4).

Delphy sees the founding principles of traditional social science disciplines as fundamentally opposed to those of feminism and women's studies:

> Knowledge which seeks to take the oppression of women as its point of departure constitutes an epistemological revolution, not just a new discipline with women as its object, and or an *ad hoc* explanation of a particular oppression. ([1975]1984: 215)

Since Delphy wrote these words, the idea that women's studies transcends disciplinary boundaries and that it challenges the epistemological bases of the conventional disciplines has become well established. Indeed, it has become fundamental to the premises which define women's studies as a specific area of intellectual endeavour in its own right. Moreover, feminist social scientists more generally have rejected the disciplinary compartmentalization of knowledge which Delphy critiques. It is now common to find feminist sociologists dealing with issues of subjectivity and sexuality on the one hand, or the economic foundations of women's lives on the other, and feminist psychologists discussing the economic, social and cultural constraints on women's lives.[1] The effect has indeed been to render human experience more intelligible.

It is also now widely accepted that women's studies produces politically engaged knowledge. For those who seek to oppose feminism's impact on academic work and to defend traditional disciplines against its critics, this political engagement is seen as evidence of the 'bias' of women's studies. Women's studies in France has been attacked by Pierre Bourdieu, a prominent member of the French intellectual establishment, on precisely these grounds (Bourdieu, 1990). Detractors such as Bourdieu sneer at knowledge constructed from the point of view of 'a dominated group . . . a "cause" which seems to be its own epistemological justification, not requiring the purely scientific work of object construction' (Bourdieu, 1990, quoted in Armengaud et al., 1995: 45–6). Delphy's point, and one which most feminist academics would endorse, is that all knowledge is a social product with political consequences and hence no knowledge is neutral. Delphy argues further that knowledge which denies this is ideological, in that it conceals the social conditions of its own production (Armengaud et al., 1995; Delphy, 1975).

Delphy, then, does not claim neutrality for women's studies. Feminist knowledge is founded upon a political understanding of women's situation as one of oppression – just as Marx's theory of capital was founded on the premise of the oppression of the proletariat:

> Oppression is one possible way of conceptualizing a given situation; and this particular conceptualization can originate only from one standpoint (that is, from one precise position in this situation): that of the

> oppressed. It is only from the point of view and life experience of women that their condition can be seen as oppression. (Delphy, 1984: 218)

Here Delphy comes close to defining what has since become known as the 'feminist standpoint' position within debates on methodology and epistemology, a position which defines feminist knowledge as knowledge produced from the point of view of the oppressed, knowledge produced by women, for women. Such knowledge necessarily challenges and lays bare the androcentrism of mainstream knowledge revealing the pretensions of its claim to objectivity. What is specific to Delphy's work is that she locates this standpoint within a materialist perspective:

> Materialist feminism is . . . an intellectual approach whose coming is crucial both for a social movement, the feminist movement, and for *knowledge*. This approach will not – cannot – be limited to a single population, to the oppression of women alone. It will not leave any aspect of reality, any domain of knowledge, any aspect of the world untouched. As the feminist movement aims at revolution in social reality, the feminist theoretical point of view must also aim at a revolution in knowledge. Each is indispensable to the other. (1984: 218; emphasis in original)

This is an ambitious project, and one which might seem overoptimistic. We are still a long way from effecting 'a revolution in social reality', since the social structures which constrain us have changed little. Western feminism has, however, had some impact, in that we have made a little progress in advancing our civil rights. To deny this, Delphy argues, is to deny the struggles of feminists, to write them out of existence. In 1980, reflecting on 10 years of the MLF (Mouvement de libération des femmes), Delphy suggested that feminism had changed the political climate. Feminism was now on the public agenda, feminist ideas were discussed, men found it necessary to make excuses for their sexism when a decade before they had not heard the word: 'This is so obvious, so ordinary, that we tend to forget that it hasn't always been like this, and that at least "at the level of discourse", we've changed our world, we've changed the world' ([1980a] 1987b: 33).

One place where this change at the level of discourse is most evident is in the academy. Here feminism is having an effect in at least some academic disciplines, notably in sociology, although the extent to which it is transforming knowledge is disputed (see, for example, Abbott, 1991; Maynard, 1990). Feminism has, however, carved out a space for itself with the growth of women's studies and a corresponding expansion in the publication of feminist work. This situation, however, raises new concerns about the production of feminist knowledge which is accessible only to the privileged few, and which may be produced and consumed by individuals who have played little part in the women's movement. One irony of this situation is that a theorist such as Delphy, whose work was inspired by her commitment to activism, may now be studied by students who have no interest in feminist politics and who read her work only in order to pass their exams. It also raises questions about the role of feminist intellectuals. Those of us with established academic careers enjoy freedoms many other women cannot contemplate. We are, for example, materially privileged in that we can earn sufficient to maintain a comfortable lifestyle without economic dependence on men. Now that feminism has entered the university in the shape of women's studies and various courses on gender, we are further privileged in that we can earn our living through the promotion of feminist ideas. This raises questions about our role in relation to the movement which made this possible for us, questions which Delphy thinks it is vital for us to confront.

Delphy has played her part in promoting women's studies in France, although it is less well established there than in many other Western countries (Armengaud et al., 1995). Delphy is not denying that women's studies are a good thing, but whether they remain so depends on 'what relationship they maintain with the political movement which instigated them and which feeds them' (Delphy, [1981b] 1984: 147). We therefore, says Delphy, have to face the problem of what role should be played by feminist intellectuals. As she points out, academia is not a neutral location in the social order. There are a number of problems here. The most obvious is the relative privilege that academic feminists enjoy over other women. The logic of a materialist argument, which recognizes the plurality of class systems is that being oppressed within one system (by our gender), does not prevent our being privileged in another, by virtue of our occupation (see Chapter 4). Moreover academic feminists are not only materially privileged, but as part of the intellectual class we acquire a stake in maintaining that class's privileged access to knowledge. How can we then ensure that 'academia serves feminism and not feminism academia?' (Delphy, 1984: 148).

Delphy draws parallels here with intellectual marxists who, at least in France, have become divorced from class struggle. The theory which they generate is often incomprehensible to anyone but other academics and is certainly not accessible to working-class activists. In part this may be due to the petit-bourgeois origins of marxist intellectuals who are not part of the class on whose behalf they claim to speak, and hence suffer a contradiction which feminist intellectuals escape. Feminist activists, unlike left activists, are fighting for their own liberation as women rather than someone else's; feminist academics are, as women, both subjects and objects of our analyses. Yet we are still members of the intellectual class – even if we are often rather lowly members of it. If we become too attached to retaining or advancing our position within that class, this creates problems for feminist analysis:

> The oppression of women could become one object of study among others, without questioning either the methods of the disciplines or the role of academia and science as privileged locations for ideological production, and hence for the maintenance of oppression – of all oppressions. (Delphy, 1984: 148–9)

This is what has happened to marxism. In the pursuit of theoretical purity and intellectual rigour, many marxist intellectuals 'believe that it is marxist *analysis* which establishes the reality of proletarian oppression, a belief which is both historically and logically absurd' (Delphy, 1984: 149; emphasis in original).[2] Delphy sees this as a perversion of Marx's intent, since Marx himself did not deduce the existence of oppression from his theory, but started from the fact of oppression which he then sought to explain: 'This perversion of revolutionary theory . . . also lies in wait for feminism . . . don't imagine that we shall be saved from danger either by magic or by our ovaries' (Delphy, 1984: 149). We certainly won't be saved by being intellectuals, she argues, because part of the objective interests of intellectuals as a class is to gather the ideas generated by social movements into its own domain, and to maintain a monopoly on that domain. Intellectuals are all too often guilty of 'the practice of making theory into the private hunting ground of the elite' (Delphy, 1980b: 81). For Delphy, theory and analysis are important in understanding how and why oppression exists, but they cannot establish the reality of oppression nor authorize revolt. Oppression is the shared experience of being unjustly treated: its basis is political not scientific. 'We must always remember that theories cannot substitute for revolt', that they themselves derive from revolt (Delphy, 1984: 150).

Feminist academics live our membership of the intellectual class every day, and are therefore all too easily sucked into accepting its mores uncritically. Delphy suggests that our best means of resisting this, of facing the contradictions of being intellectuals, is our anger. It is not just a matter of abstract political commitment, but of maintaining the sense of outrage and injustice which inspired that commitment. We need this in order to avoid becoming party to a system which withholds useful knowledge from those who need it most. Academic knowledge is frequently incomprehensible to outsiders. Its production is at present 'inseparable from the production of a *learned* discourse which is defined in opposition to "popular" language – i.e. that of the group which is dominated' (Delphy, 1984: 151). Academia therefore excludes the oppressed from intellectual tools which might enable them to think about their oppression. Delphy gives the example of critiques of male academic sexism which we construct with the intent of furthering feminism. But if these critiques are to be of any use to feminist activists, if they are to help to demystify patriarchal claims to 'truth' about women, they have to be understandable. If we make them understandable we will be disdained by our male colleagues; if we construct them in suitably intellectual language we may be able to convict the men concerned of sexism in the eyes of the academic community, but we thereby enter into a more fundamental complicity with them, 'a complicity based on the exclusion of all non-intellectuals, in which group are to be found the majority of feminists' (Delphy, 1984: 151). Anyone who has had much to do with academic feminism will realize that Delphy's fears are well-founded. There is much theory now being generated which is incomprehensible not only to the average feminist activist but also to many with academic training. This situation also, she argues, feeds an unfortunate but understandable anti-intellectualism among feminist activists 'who refuse all theory without realizing that, for better or worse, their practice always incorporates a theory, whether explicit or not' (Delphy, 1980b: 81).

For Delphy, as we have seen, there is no such thing as a neutral science, knowledge is always constructed from a particular perspective. Hence reactionary analyses are not 'wrong', but may be perfectly correct from the point of view of dominant groups: 'An analysis only has value from a class position, insofar as it serves this position' (Delphy, 1984: 150). We need to be constantly aware that it is a myth that any knowledge is pure, scientific and neutral. If a feminist analysis becomes mystified as 'knowledge' in this way, then we betray feminism. The only reason that we can study women's oppression is because millions of women 'suffer in the flesh' from that oppression: 'To make this a mere academic problem is to deny, worse to insult, this suffering' (Delphy, 1984: 152). The only way to avoid this, Delphy says, is to keep reminding ourselves that the suffering is the only valid reason for studying women's oppression and that the only value of theory is if it can contribute to ending this suffering.

We tend to see feminism's admission to the realms of academic knowledge as progress, an indication that it is taken seriously. It allows for rigorous dispassionate analysis. But this, says Delphy, is a 'devil's trap' (1984: 151). It means succumbing to the myth of science, and protects us against our own anger. For Delphy it is all important to hang on to our anger: it is what connects us to our class as women. We must remember that we too are women, that whatever the protection offered by our status as intellectuals, we are often humiliated and oppressed. We should not see our anger as an encumbrance, something that stands in the way of our intellectual work, but as the guarantee that our intellectual work will continue to serve the women's movement:

> Our only weapon against the potential treason written into our status as intellectuals is precisely our anger. The only guarantee that we will not, as intellectuals, be traitors to our class, is our awareness of being, ourselves, women, of being among those whose oppression we analyse. The only basis for this consciousness is our revolt; and the only foundation for this revolt is our anger. (Delphy, [1981b] 1984: 153)

In conclusion: an assessment of Delphy's influence

Although Delphy has always been very insistent on promoting materialist radical feminist analysis, and indeed implies strongly that materialism is the *only* perspective that can advance the feminist cause, she does not advance a vanguardist view of the women's movement. That is to say, she does not claim that materialist radical feminists have a monopoly on feminist truth. Where feminism is concerned, she says, we must be nominalist (Delphy, 1991a); in other words, if a woman calls herself a feminist, we must accept her as such. She knows from her experience of activism that it is possible to work across differences, and has commented that some of the differences which were so divisive in the early days of the MLF, particularly those between radical feminists and the 'class struggle' tendency, are now less important. As socialist feminists have become more attuned to the need to organize autonomously as women, some of these differences have lessened. Moreover, now that the women's movement is more fragmented, Delphy feels that socialist feminists' contribution to grass-roots activism should be recognized.[3] While she is capable of scathing attacks on those she sees as undermining the feminist struggle, she is far more tolerant than many of reformist feminism. She has said that she does not feel that we can draw an exclusionary circle around 'pure' feminism and condemn all else. To do so is to deny the different routes women take into feminism, the varying ways in which consciousness is raised and the limits of what is possible for some women (Delphy, 1980a, 1987b). Feminism should be capable of encompassing all women, not only those with the most 'advanced' analysis. Ultimately, however, she feels that we need a sound analysis of our oppression if we are to fight against it successfully.[4]

Since her early involvement in the women's movement, Delphy has identified herself as a radical feminist as well as a materialist. What was at stake in this identification was a commitment to an autonomous women's movement and an analysis of patriarchy as a system of male power through which men benefited from the oppression of women. Most radical feminists would agree with these basic premises, but beyond this they differ in their approaches to theorizing women's oppression. In most summaries of feminist theory available to students, however, the diversity of radical feminist perspectives is ignored or played down, and frequently its materialist variant goes unmentioned. Mary Maynard (1995) contends that the root of the problem is that most theory texts take as their starting point 'the big three' feminist perspectives – radical feminism, socialist or marxist feminism and liberal feminism – even if they then add on other feminisms. Maynard suggests that Delphy is an example of a theorist who does not fit this oversimplified, ahistorical system of classification. In the first place these categories imply that marxist and radical feminism are discrete, opposing positions, with no common concerns and no dialogue between them. Because Delphy uses marxist methods and addresses issues which are more often associated with marxist feminists – such as domestic labour and class – she is not easily placed in the box marked 'radical feminism'. Moreover, more than any other form of feminism, radical feminism suffers from stereotypical misrepresentation. Generally it is portrayed as essentialist, as founded on the assumption that men and women are fundamentally, innately different. Individual, unrepresentative theorists such as Shulamith Firestone (1972) are singled out to back these assumptions. Alternatively feminists who have written on pornography or rape, such as Susan Brownmiller (1976) or Andrea Dworkin (1981), are used to suggest that radical feminists are primarily or solely concerned with male violence.[5] Once again, Delphy does not slot easily into this construction of radical feminism, since she is rigorously anti-essentialist and has not devoted herself to the study of violence.[6]

As a result of the ways in which feminist theory has become packaged in women's studies texts, Delphy's ideas do not circulate as widely as they might. Nonetheless, she has established a place for herself as one of the key thinkers of second-wave feminism. Her prominence as a feminist theorist was probably greatest in the late 1970s and early 1980s, the period when she was engaged in debate with her marxist feminist critics. She has, however, continued to influence much feminist sociological work, especially in Britain.

In the 1990s, materialist analyses are not particularly fashionable in academic feminist circles. Somewhat prematurely, and I would say groundlessly, a theoretical tradition little more than twenty years old has already been declared by some to be outmoded. Over the last decade many of those who once saw themselves as marxist feminists have turned their backs on materialist analysis in favour of a focus on language, discourse and representation. This includes some of Delphy's erstwhile marxist critics, such as Michèle Barrett, who has characterized this trend as a 'cultural turn', a shift in the objects of feminist analysis from 'things' to 'words' (1992). This has also signalled a move away from sociologically informed perspectives within women's studies towards those deriving from literary and cultural studies. By the early 1980s, many marxist feminists were already arguing that rather than being rooted, like class, in relations of production, women's subordination was primarily ideological. At first, this was accomplished through an Althusserian framework drawing in the arguments of Lacan and Lévi-Strauss, an approach pioneered by Juliet Mitchell (1975). In part this was a response to the perceived failure of marxism to deal with issues of subjectivity and sexuality. Psychoanalysis, in particular, became attractive because it seemed to fill the gaps left by Marx, hence marxist feminists grafted a non-materialist argument on to marxism (Delphy, 1981b). Subsequently, Foucault's work and that of other postmodernists were looked to as a means of theorizing diversity among women. This entailed the abandonment of analyses of the material conditions of women's lives, the denial of any overarching systems of power, and a move towards a focus on culture and the discursive construction of difference.[7]

At this stage the continued defence of marxism's relevance was left to those materialist feminists whose affiliations were closer to radical than to marxist feminism. Those once castigated for being insufficiently marxist now found themselves charged with clinging on to an outmoded, modernist, foundationalist discourse incapable of coping with the complexities of gender relations in a post-modern, post-colonial world. Whether in fact materialism is incapable of dealing with such complexities is a moot point (see, for example, Walby, 1992). It is true that some materialists, Delphy included, have given little attention to the construction of racial differences and that their analyses have focused primarily on white

Western women. But this is by no means true of all materialist feminists (see, for example, Guillaumin, 1995). It seems to me that the material foundations and consequences of institutionalized racism, the heritage of centuries of slavery, colonialism and imperialism and the continued international division of labour, are at least as important as culturally constituted difference. We live our lives now within a global system characterized by extremely stark material inequalities. The material oppression suffered by women has not gone away, and for many women in the world their situation is worsening. The continued vitality of approaches which deal with such inequalities is crucial for feminist politics and theory.

I would not like to give the impression that materialist analysis has disappeared. On the contrary, within feminist sociology it is alive and well. Here feminists continue to demonstrate that material factors shape women's lives in determinate ways. Delphy's influence on sociology, though, has been greater in Britain than in her native France. In part this difference is attributable to the strength of Women's Studies in Britain and the impact which feminist sociologists have been able to have on their discipline (Maynard, 1990). However, this is not to say that Delphy's ideas are without influence within French sociology – the materialist perspective she helped to develop is well represented among feminist sociologists there. This is evident in many of the studies of rural French families drawn on in *Familiar Exploitation* (Delphy and Leonard, 1992). Delphy has also been an active participant in debates on gender and social sex in France (see Adkins and Leonard, 1995). Feminists in general, though, face an uphill struggle within French academia, with male sociologists either ignoring feminist scholarship or producing anti-feminist work. Some, for example, still maintain that women's location within families is an immutable fact of life (see Armengaud et al., 1995: 48–9).

In Britain, feminist sociology is not without its detractors and there are some areas where its impact remains slight. Nonetheless, here most sociologists do acknowledge its existence and it has been incorporated into undergraduate courses and introductory textbooks. Materialist feminist ideas found favour in British sociology in part because of its strong tradition of empirical and theoretical work on social inequalities and its history of engagement with marxism.[8] Hence many of Delphy's central ideas have become woven into debates within British sociology. It is now widely accepted, for example, that families are fundamentally inegalitarian and that conventional theories of class are flawed by their lack of attention to gender (see Maynard, 1990). Materialist feminism, whether derived directly from Delphy or mediated by Walby, is also evident in much research on gender segregation in the labour market (for example, Adkins, 1995; Witz, 1992).

Delphy's direct influence, as we might expect, has been greatest in sociological work on families. Janet Finch's analysis of wives' contributions to their husbands' occupation has already been discussed (see Chapter 3), and more recently she has widened her focus to encompass kin ties and inheritance (Finch, 1983, 1989). Members of the Resources within Households Study Group (see Brannen and Wilson, 1987) have provided a great deal of empirical backing for Delphy's analysis of consumption within families. The work of this group has conclusively demonstrated that 'while sharing a common address family members do not necessarily share a common standard of living' (Graham, 1987: 221). One such study, Nickie Charles and Marion Kerr's research on family food consumption, confirms not only the inegalitarian nature of resource distribution, but also its relation to the relative power and status of family members. Charles and Kerr have also gone some way towards exploring some of the interconnections between the economic and emotional aspects of family relationships and between material inequalities and familial ideology (Charles, 1990; Charles and Kerr, 1988). Delphy's ideas are also proving relevant to a new generation of sociologists. For example, Jo Van Every (1995) found in Delphy and Leonard's (1992) analysis a means of making sense of her data on heterosexual women seeking anti-sexist living arrangements; Lisa Adkins (1995) has drawn on both Delphy and Walby in exploring the interconnections between family and labour market. The extent to which Delphy is now recognized as a major sociological thinker is evident in the place she occupies in recent mainstream (and male authored) texts on sociological theory and methods originating in Britain and Australia (for example, Harvey, 1990; Waters, 1994).

There is, however, a tendency in some feminist writing today to assume that theories which emerged in the first decade of second-wave feminism have now been superseded, and that feminists who continue to work within these theoretical frameworks are no longer producing relevant work. In particular, feminist postmodernists constantly warn us against these older theoretical traditions, implying that they claim to have discovered the ultimate cause of women's oppression or that they assume universal applicability for theories generated from a particular historical and social location (see, for example, Flax, 1990). We should be sceptical of accepting these charges without verifying them for ourselves, for these accusations are not always just. Delphy's early work certainly cannot be characterized in this way. She has been consistently critical of attempts to construct totalizing theories of women's oppression and has sought only to illuminate specific aspects of it. Similarly, she has always been sceptical of trans-historical, universalistic explanations. She has certainly never claimed to have produced some absolute truth, but rather an analysis from a particular, politically engaged, position. Nonetheless, her materialism does presuppose a 'real' world outside and prior to discourse, and in this sense will always be irreconcilable with much postmodernist thinking. There are signs, though, that some feminists are on the retreat from the extreme anti-materialist end of postmodernism, are edging towards accepting the existence of such 'totalities' as capitalism, patriarchy and racism and arguing for a more materially grounded form of discourse analysis (see, for example, Hennessy, 1993). If this becomes a widespread trend, it could presage a resurgence of materialist analysis.

Just as Delphy claimed that Marx's materialism was his most important legacy, so I would argue that it is Delphy's reworking of that method which constitutes her most important contribution to feminism. Of course there are gaps and omissions in her analysis – she would never claim otherwise. In the course of this book I have identified two main ones. First, she says little about racial divisions and their intersection with gender divisions,[9] an issue which has now become, rightly, far more central to feminism. Second, there is, as yet, no materialist feminist analysis of subjectivity and hence no viable alternative to psychoanalysis. In neither case, however, do I consider these areas beyond the reach of materialist analysis.

Delphy's intellectual strength lies in the production of original ideas and conceptual frameworks, formulated as tightly argued articles and sharp, impassioned polemics rather than as lengthy elaborations of her ideas. Hence the total volume of work she has produced is rather less than one might expect from a theorist of such stature.[10] In assessing her ideas, though, it must be remembered that we are not dealing with a finished body of work. Delphy continues to write and remains engaged with current feminist debates. All her work, from her earliest writings to the most recent, addresses issues which feminism cannot afford to ignore. Most of her work to date falls into two main areas. The writings which made her name as a theorist analysed women's work within families and the relations of dependence within which this work is carried out. Despite all the recent rhetoric about the diversity of family forms and women's increasing participation in the labour market, most women in Western societies still marry, still do the bulk of the housework and still, because they do not enter into paid work on the same terms as men, carry out this work as men's dependants. Housework may no longer be at the centre of theoretical debates, but it remains a central issue in many women's lives. Second, Delphy has devoted much attention to the social basis of gender division itself. The fact of that division, however it is theorized, is, and must remain, fundamental to feminist analysis. As long as the material inequalities Delphy has worked on persist – and it seems they will be with us for a long time to come – her work will retain its relevance for feminism and for sociology.

Notes

1. To take just one example, Ann Phoenix's study of young mothers illustrates the willingness of feminist researchers to cross disciplinary boundaries. Phoenix is a psychologist. Where a traditional, pre-feminist, psychologist would have considered early motherhood in terms of individual subjectivity, possibly individual pathology, and looked at such issues as the family backgrounds of such young women, Phoenix takes a much broader view. She deals with such issues as the economic and social constraints on young women's lives, the impact of racism and the cultural and political construction of early motherhood as a social problem. She also treats young mothers as active social agents, making choices about their life strategies in the context of the constraints they face (Phoenix, 1991).

2. One example of the sort of marxism Delphy is referring to here is the work of Nicos Poulantzas (1973) who defines the working class in such a way as to render it a very small minority of the population. To be working class one has to be a productive worker, directly producing surplus value, a manual worker and have not even a minor supervisory role over other workers. This satisfies the criteria for marxist purity that Poulantzas sets up, but it excludes from the proletariat many oppressed workers (for example, cleaners, refuse collectors, shop workers) who in terms of the spirit of marxism might be thought to be proletarians. For a critique see Wright (1973).

3. The above comments are from my interview with Delphy, August 1993.

4. Personal correspondence with Delphy.

5. These writers are themselves often misrepresented as unproblematically essentialist and as arguing that rape or pornography is the sole cause of women's oppression.

6. She has however, been involved in grass-roots campaigns around rape and was involved in producing polemical leaflets on this issue (see Chapter 1).

7. The content of such journals as *mf* and *Feminist Review* provide illustrations of these shifts, as does the theoretical trajectory followed by Barrett herself.

8. This might help to explain why materialist feminism has less purchase in the USA, despite a thriving feminist sociology there.

9. This lays her open to charges of ethnocentrism (see Maynard, 1990, 1995).

10. Most of Delphy's work was originally published as articles, some of the most important of which have been collected together in *Close to Home* (Delphy, 1984). The only full, book length exposition of the theories she has developed is her collaborative work with Leonard, *Familiar Exploitation* (1992). At the time of going to press, new collections of Delphy's work, in both French and English, are planned.

Bibliographical Sources

These bibliographical sources are organized into three sections. The first comprises an annotated bibliography of Delphy's works published in English. The second section lists all Delphy's works in French. In the third section I provide a short annotated bibliography of some of the more useful secondary sources on French feminism.

1. Works by Delphy available in English

Books

The Main Enemy. London: Women's Research and Resources Centre, 1977.

The pamphlet, edited and introduced by Diana Leonard, was the first publication to make Delphy's work widely available in English. The title article, published in French in 1970, is Delphy's original formulation of her theories on the domestic mode of production (see Chapter 3). This piece, translated by Lucy ap Roberts, had previously been circulated in mimeod form. In addition the pamphlet contains two translations by Diana Leonard: 'Proto-feminism and anti-feminism' and a transcript of a debate on feminist politics between Delphy and Danièle Leger. 'Proto-feminism and anti-feminism' is a critique of Annie Leclerc's *Parole de femme*, in which Delphy attacks Leclerc's naturalistic and idealist assumptions. This article is one of the earliest expositions of Delphy's anti-essentialist position, which is fundamental to her materialism (see Chapters 2 and 5). Delphy's debate with Leger illustrates the differences between materialist and marxist feminists' approaches to domestic labour and to class politics.

'The main enemy' and 'Proto-feminism and anti-feminism' were later included in *Close to Home.*

Close to Home: A Materialist Analysis of Women's Oppression. London: Hutchinson, 1984.

This collection of Delphy's major early works, edited and translated by Diana Leonard, contains a new introduction by Delphy and ten other articles, three of which are only available in English in this collection. The contents of these three are outlined here; the other articles are dealt with separately.

'Housework or domestic work' is a further development of Delphy's analysis of women's unpaid work, and examines the inconsistencies in conventional social scientific distinctions between productive and unproductive work and between occupational work and housework. Delphy argues against empiricist definitions of housework as a set of tasks and for a theoretical conceptualization of domestic work (or familial work) – the unpaid work undertaken by women within domestic or family relations of production (see Chapter 3).

'Our friends and ourselves: the hidden foundations of various pseudo-feminist accounts', is a polemic against those men who claim to support feminism while undermining it. The article deals with some of the assumptions entailed in asserting the primacy of class struggle over feminist struggle, exposing the misogyny underlying attacks made on bourgeois women in the name of class solidarity (see Chapter 4).

'Patriarchy, feminism and their intellectuals', offers a critique of those feminist theories of patriarchy which rest on essentialist assumptions (for example, the psychoanalytic perspective of Juliet Mitchell and the approach of British revolutionary feminists). The article raises questions about the status of feminist theory and the contradictions faced by academic feminists (see Chapter 6).

Delphy's introduction to *Close to Home* explains how she came to develop her ideas and outlines the basic premises of her materialism, covering the domestic mode of production, her position on patriarchy, her methodology, her opposition to naturalism and her conceptualization of gender and sex classes. A useful preface by Leonard situates Delphy's work for English readers and places it in the context of developments in both French and Anglophone feminist theory.

Familiar Exploitation: A New Analysis of Marriage in Contemporary Western Societies. Oxford: Polity, 1992.

Co-authored with Diana Leonard, and the product of a long collaboration with her, this book represents the fullest development of Delphy's theories on the exploitation of women's unpaid labour (see Chapter 3). As well as synthesizing and building upon Delphy's earlier work, the book contains some new elements: a thorough summary and critique of marxist and marxist feminist perspectives, a discussion of the variety of work performed by wives and an interpretation of empirical data from France and Britain in terms of Delphy and Leonard's theoretical framework.

Individually authored articles

'Continuities and discontinuities in marriage and divorce', in Diana Leonard Barker and Sheila Allen (eds), *Sexual Divisions and Society: Process and Change.* London: Tavistock, 1976.

Here Delphy analyses divorce and marriage as interrelated institutions. Conceptualizing marriage as a labour contract, she discusses the interrelationship between women's disadvantage in the labour market and their exploitation in the home. She considers women's responsibility for childcare both within marriage and after divorce in terms of men's individual and collective appropriation of women's labour (see Chapter 3).

This piece is included in *Close to Home* and was subsequently republished as 'Is there marriage after divorce?' in D. Leonard and S. Allen (eds), *Sexual Divisions Revisited.*

'Sharing the same table: consumption and the family', translated by Diana Leonard, in C.C. Harris (ed.), *The Sociology of the Family: New Directions for Britain.* Sociological Review Monograph No. 28. University of Keele, 1979.

This article challenges the widespread assumption that consumption within families is organized on an equitable, collective basis, contending that, on the contrary, it is ordered in terms of hierarchies of gender and generation (see Chapter 3).

A revised translation was published in *Close to Home.*

'A materialist feminism is possible', translated by Diana Leonard, *Feminist Review,* No. 4, 1980.

This is Delphy's response to her marxist feminist critics, particularly to Barrett and McIntosh, whose critique of her work was published in the first issue of *Feminist Review*. She counters the claim that she is insufficiently marxist by arguing that it is her critics who misconstrue Marx's intent. She maintains that marxist feminists' opposition to her perspective is founded on a wish to exonerate men from any responsibility for the oppression of women (see Chapter 3).

A shorter version is included in *Close to Home*.

'Feminist glimmerings in Eastern Europe', *Feminist Issues*, 1(1), 1980.

A report of a conference in Belgrade in 1978, the first feminist conference to be held in what was then Yugoslavia.

'Women in stratification studies', translated by Helen Roberts, in Helen Roberts (ed.), *Doing Feminist Research*. Routledge and Kegan Paul, 1981.

Starting from a critique of sociologists' inconsistent treatment of women in stratification studies, Delphy argues for a radical reconceptualization of class which would recognize the specific class situation of women within domestic relations of production.

A much clearer translation by Diana Leonard is included in *Close to Home*.

'For a materialist feminism', *Feminist Issues* , 1 (2): 69–76, 1981.

Here Delphy offers a critique of conventional social scientific knowledge and argues for the production of feminist knowledge centred on women's oppression (see Chapter 6). She also argues against attempts to reconcile marxism and psychoanalysis and for a materialist perspective on subjectivity (see Chapters 2 and 5).

A short extract is reproduced in E. Marks and I. de Courtivron (eds) *New French Feminisms*. Brighton: Harvester, 1981. A better translation, by Diana Leonard, is included in *Close to Home*.

'Women's liberation in France: the tenth year', *Feminist Issues* , 1 (2): 103–12, 1981.

In this article Delphy assesses the gains made by the French women's movement in the ten years following its emergence. She stresses the importance of recording our own history, lest the lessons of feminism be forgotten (see Chapter 6). She illustrates this by looking at the way in which women's autonomous campaigning around abortion was written out of history only a few years after the liberalization of abortion laws in France (see Chapter 1).

A translation by Claire Duchen is included in her *French Connections* (1987).

'Proto-feminism and anti-feminism', in Tovil Moi (ed.), *French Feminist Thought*. Oxford: Blackwell, 1987.

This is a reprint of Diana Leonard's translation, previously published in *The Main Enemy* and in *Close to Home*.

'Women's liberation: the tenth year', translated by Claire Duchen, in C. Duchen (ed.), *French Connections*. London: Hutchinson, 1987.

Previously published in *Feminist Issues* (see above).

'Patriarchy, domestic mode of production, gender and class', in C. Nelson and L. Grossberg (eds), *Marxism and the Interpretation of Culture*. London: Macmillan, 1988.

This article covers substantially the same ground as Delphy's introduction to *Close to Home* (see above).

'Is there marriage after divorce?' in Diana Leonard and Shiela Allen (eds), *Sexual Divisions Revisited*. London: Macmillan, 1991.

A reprint of 'Continuities and discontinuities in marriage and divorce'.

'Mothers' Union?', translated by Diana Leonard in *Trouble and Strife*, 24: 12–19, 1992.

This is an abridged version of 'Changing women in a changing Europe: is difference the future for feminism?' which was subsequently published in *Women's Studies International Forum*.

'Rethinking sex and gender', *Women's Studies International Forum*, 16 (1): 1–9, 1993.

In this article Delphy provides a useful critical overview of the development of the concept of gender as it developed from the earlier concept of sex roles. Delphy goes on to elaborate her own theory of gender, arguing that not just the content of gender, but the fact of gender division itself, is socially constructed and that gender difference is the product of patriarchal hierarchy (see Chapter 5).

'Changing women in a changing Europe: is difference the future for feminism?', *Women's Studies International Forum*, 27 (2): 187–201, 1994.

Here Delphy confronts what she sees as a worrying trend in feminist thinking – the tendency to seek specific rights for women on the basis of motherhood, which she argues derives from essentialist conceptions of women's difference. She examines instances of this in feminist campaigns around reproductive technology, in feminist reconstructions of evolution and in writings about motherhood more generally. She concludes that these maternal demands have more to do with defending women's 'ownership' of children than with women's liberation (see Chapters 3 and 5).

'The invention of French feminism: an essential move', *Yale French Studies*, 87, 1995 Special Issue: 'Another Look, Another Woman: the Reconstitution of French Feminism'.

The Anglo-American construction of 'French Feminism' has, Delphy argues, little to do with feminism in France. She challenges this misrepresentation, arguing that it constitutes a form of imperialism which ignores the views of feminists in France and promotes anti-feminist thinkers as feminists (see Chapter 2).

Collaboratively written articles

Questions Féministes Collective, 'Variations on common themes' (editorial to the first issue of *QF*), translated by Yvonne Rochette-Ozzello, in E. Marks and I. de Courtivron (eds), *New French Feminisms*. Brighton: Harvester, 1981.

This editorial sets out the basic premises of French radical feminism. Although it is collectively written, the individual authors of particular sections are identified by initials. The passage bearing the initials CD and MP was co-written by Christine Delphy and Monique Plaza and deals mainly with the issue of gender, attacking the naturalistic assumptions of the 'neo-femininity' current in France and asserting that men and women are social, not natural, categories (see Chapters 1 and 5).

Nouvelles Questions Féministes Collective, 'A movement for all women' (extracts from editorial to *Nouvelles Questions Féministes*, 1), translated by Sophie Laws in *Trouble and Strife*, 2: 33–4, 1984.

Delphy was a part of the editorial collective which here sets out the position of the journal, following the split in the *QF* collective over the issue of radical lesbianism (see Chapter 1).

Reprinted in C. Duchen (ed.), *French Connections*. London: Hutchinson, 1987, pp. 81–3.

Féministes Révolutionnaires, 'Patriarchal justice and the threat of rape', in dusty rhodes and Sandra McNeill (eds), *Women Against Violence Against Women*. London: Onlywomen Press, 1985.

This is a translation of a polemical leaflet, drafted by Delphy and produced by the radical feminist group in which she was involved, at the launch of an anti-rape campaign in 1976 (see Chapter 1). It argues that rape is a form of social control in which the patriarchal state colludes with rapists to reinforce women's subordination.

Christine Delphy and Diana Leonard, 'Class analysis, gender analysis and the family', in Rosemary Crompton and Michael Mann (eds), *Gender and Stratification*. Oxford: Polity, 1986.

This is a further critique of sociological work on class, exposing the patriarchal reasoning and naturalistic assumptions implicit in much of this work. It focuses on the problems posed by treating class as rooted in the occupational hierarchy and the family as the unit of stratification, particularly of differentiating between direct holders of class positions and non-holders (dependants). This article also considers the role of hereditary transmission, itself a gendered process, in the constitution of classes (see Chapter 4).

Françoise Armengaud, Ghaïss Jasser and Christine Delphy, 'Liberty, equality . . . but most of all, fraternity', *Trouble and Strife*, 31: 43–9, 1995.

Feminists in France found themselves excluded from the preparation of the official French report to the Fourth World Conference on Women in Beijing in 1995. The report was compiled by a committee of three men and one woman. This article explains the background to this situation, pointing to the attacks on feminist scholarship made by prominent male intellectuals, the precarious situation of women's studies in France and men's attempts to monopolize studies on women within a reactionary, pro-family framework.

Articles by Christine Delphy published in French

'Le patrimonie et la double circulation des biens dans l'espace économique et le temps familial', *Revue Française de Sociologie*, 10, 1969.
'L'ennemi principal', *Partisans*, 54–5, 1970.
'Mariage et divorce: l'impasse à double face', *Les Temps Modernes*, mai 1974.
'Pour un féminisme matérialiste', *L'Arc*, avril 1975.

'La famille et la fonction de consommation', *Cahiers Internationaux de Sociologie*, été 1975.

'Proto-féminisme et anti-féminisme', *Les Temps Modernes*, mai 1976.

'La transmission du statut à Chardonneret', *Revue d'Ethnologie Française*, 4 (1–2), 1976.

'Les femmes dans les études de stratification sociale', in A. Michel (ed.), *Femmes, sexisme et sociétés*. Paris: PUF, 1977.

'Nos amis et nous, des fondements réels de quelques discours pseudo-féministes', *Questions Féministes*, novembre 1977.

'Travail ménager ou travail domestique?', in A. Michel (ed.), *Les femmes dans la société marchande*, Paris: PUF, 1978.

'Libération des femmes an 10', *Questions Féministes*, 7, 1980.

'Le patriarchat, le féminisme et leurs intellectuelles', *Nouvelles Questions Féministes*, 2, octobre 1981.

Un féminisme matérialiste est possible', *Nouvelles Questions Féministes*, 4, automne 1982.

'Agriculture et travail domestique: la réponse de la bergère à Engels', *Nouvelles Questions Féministes*, 5, printemps 1983.

'Les femmes et l'Etat', *Nouvelles Questions Féministes*, 7, printemps 1984.

'Contribution au débat sur l'avortement', *Déviance et Société*, 14 (4), 1990.

'La revendication maternelle', in L. Vandelac, F. Descarries and G. Gagnon (eds), *Du privé au politique: la maternité et le travail des femmes comme enjeux des rapports de sexes*. Montreal: Actes de l'ACFAS, UQUAM, 1990.

'Liberation des femmes ou droits corporatistes des mères?', *Nouvelles Questions Féministes*, 16–17–18, 1991.

'Les origines du mouvement de libération des femmes en France', *Nouvelles Questions Féministes*, 16–17–18, 1991.

'Penser le genre: Quels problems?', in M.-C. Hurtig, M. Kail and H. Rouch (eds), *Sex et genre: De la hierarchie entre les sexes*, Paris: Editions du Centre National de la Reserche Scientifique, 1991.

'Du contrat d'union civile, du mariage, du concubinage et de la personne, surtout féminine', *Nouvelles Questions Féministes*, 13 (1), 1992.

'Égalité, équivalence et équité: la position de l'État français au regard du droit international', *Nouvelles Questions Féministes*, 16 (1): 5–58, 1995.

Secondary sources on French feminism: a short annotated bibliography

There are numerous works on French feminism, some of which deal only with the Anglo-American version. I have included here only those which offer a broader perspective on either the French women's movement or feminist theory in France, or which cover events and debates in which Delphy was involved.

Adkins, Lisa and Leonard, Diana (eds) (1995) *Sex in Question: French Feminism*. London: Taylor and Francis.

A collection of French materialist feminist writings on gender and sex, including work previously unavailable in English. The volume has a lengthy introduction contextualizing materialist feminism for English-speaking readers and explaining its central tenets.

Beauvoir, Simone de (1985) 'Feminism – alive, well and in constant danger', translated by Magda Bogin and Robin Morgan, in Robin Morgan (ed.), *Sisterhood is Global*. Harmondsworth: Penguin. pp. 232–8.

From a radical feminist perspective close to that of Delphy herself, Beauvoir gives an overview of the history of the MLF up to 1982 and of the tendencies within it, plus an assessment of the movement's achievements and its status in the 1980s.

Duchen, Claire (1984) 'What's the French for political lesbian?', *Trouble and Strife*, 2: 24–34.

A short article plus a selection of translated extracts from French publications dealing with the debates about political/radical lesbianism and the split in the *Questions Féministes* collective.

Duchen, Claire (1986) *Feminism in France: From May '68 to Mitterand.* London: Routledge.

The most comprehensive account of the history of the MLF available in English. The book covers both the history of feminist activism in France and the development of theoretical and political debates.

Duchen, Claire (ed.) (1987) *French Connections: Voices from the Women's Movement in France*. London: Hutchinson.

This selection of writings from the MLF complements *Feminism in France*. It includes work representing all the tendencies within the French movement.

Kaplan, Gisela (1992) *Contemporary Western European Feminism*, London: UCL Press; Sydney: Allen & Unwin.

This book includes one chapter on France and the Netherlands. The information on France is largely derived from previously published sources, but it does include some more recent information not available elsewhere.

Marks, Elaine and Courtivron, Isabelle de (eds) (1981) *New French Feminisms: An Anthology*. Brighton: Harvester.

A well established collection, but one which has contributed to the misrepresentation of 'French feminism'. Almost all the work included deals with language and psychoanalysis. It does, however, contain the editorial from the first issue of *Questions Féministes* and a short extract from Delphy's 'For a materialist feminism'. It also has a lengthy introduction giving background information on the women's movement in France, some of which is useful – including a historical chronology of the MLF up to 1978. Even here, however, radical feminism's contribution is played down or ignored.

Moi, Toril (ed.) (1987) *French Feminist Thought: A Reader*. Oxford: Blackwell.

This collection attempts to provide a more balanced view of French feminism, but still gives more attention to the Anglo-American version than is warranted. It does however make substantial extracts from Anne Tristan and Annie de Pisan's *Histoires du MLF* available to English readers (see pages 33–69). This covers the early history of the MLF and was written by one of Delphy's then close associates, Anne Zelensky (aka Anne Tristan). Delphy is the 'Christine' referred to here, 'Monique' is Monique Wittig, 'Mano' is Emannuèle de Lesseps, 'Antionette' is Antionette Fouque.

Sauter-Bailliet, Teresia (1981) 'The feminist movement in France', *Women's Studies International Quarterly*, 4 (4): 409–20.

This article deals briefly with the early history of the MLF, describes tendencies within it and discusses campaigns around abortion and rape in the 1970s. The account of the FMA (a mixed group in which Delphy was involved) is inaccurate in suggesting that its women members vanished into left politics. For a better account of the FMA see the extract from Tristan and Pisan in Moi (1987).

Smyth, Ailbhe (1983) 'Contemporary French feminism: an annotated shortlist of recent works', *Hecate*, 9: 203–36.

An extensive annotated bibliography of work by and about French feminists up to 1982. Although most of the sources cited are in French, the annotations give a good sense of the breadth of French feminist writing in the 1970s and early 1980s, which itself counteracts the narrow view of it promulgated in the English speaking world. The works cited are organized under a number of headings including history, education, work, politics, abortion, violence and so on.

References

Abbott, Pamela (1991) 'Feminist perspectives in sociology', in J. Aaron and S. Walby (eds), *Out of the Margins: Women's Studies in the Nineties*. London: The Falmer Press. pp.181–90.

Acker, Joan (1973) 'Women and social stratification: a case of intellectual sexism', *American Journal of Sociology*, 78: 936–45.

Acker, Joan (1980) 'Women and stratification: a review of recent literature', *Contemporary Sociology*, 9: 25–39.

Adams, Parveen (1989) 'Of female bondage', in T. Brennan (ed.), *Between Feminism and Psychoanalysis*. London: Routledge. pp. 247–65.

Adkins, Lisa (1995) *Gendered Work: Sexuality, Family and the Labour Market*. Milton Keynes: Open University Press.

Adkins, Lisa and Leonard, Diana (eds) (1995) *Sex in Question: French Feminism*. London: Taylor and Francis.

Adlam, Diana (1979) 'Into the shadows', *Red Rag*, 14.

Afshar, Haleh (1989) 'Gender roles and the "moral economy of kin" among Pakistani women in West Yorkshire', *New Community*, 15 (2): 211–25.

Armengaud, Françoise, Jasser, Ghaïss and Delphy, Christine (1995) 'Liberty, equality . . . but most of all fraternity', *Trouble and Strife*, 31: 43–9.

Barker, Diana Leonard and Allen, Sheila (eds) (1976) *Sexual Divisions and Society: Process and Change*. London: Tavistock.

Barrett, Michèle (1980) *Women's Oppression Today*. London: Verso.

Barrett, Michèle (1988) 'Comment' (on Delphy) in C. Nelson and L. Grossberg (eds), *Marxism and the Interpretation of Culture*. London: Macmillan. pp.268–9.

Barrett, Michèle (1991) *The Politics of Truth: From Marx to Foucault*. Oxford: Polity.

Barrett, Michèle (1992) 'Words and things: materialism and method in contemporary feminist analysis', in M. Barrett and A. Phillips (eds), *Destabalizing Theory: Contemporary Feminist Debates*. Oxford: Polity. pp. 201–19.

Barrett, Michèle and McIntosh, Mary (1979) 'Christine Delphy: towards a materialist feminism', *Feminist Review*, 1: 95–106.

Barrett, Michèle and McIntosh, Mary (1982) *The Anti-Social Family.* London: Verso.

Baxter, Sue and Raw, Geoff (1988) 'Fast food, fettered work: Chinese women in the ethnic catering industry', in S. Westwood and P. Bhachu (eds), *Enterprising Women: Ethnicity, Economy and Gender Relations.* London: Routledge. pp. 58–75.

Beauvoir, Simone de (1949) *Le Deuxième Sexe* (The Second Sex). Paris: Gallimard.

Beauvoir, Simone de (1985) 'Feminism – alive, well and in constant danger', translated by Magda Bogin and Robin Morgan, in Robin Morgan (ed.), *Sisterhood is Global.* Harmondsworth: Penguin. pp. 232–8.

Beechey, Veronica (1979) 'On patriarchy', *Feminist Review,* 3: 66–82.

Benston, Margaret (1969) 'The political economy of women's liberation', *Monthly Review,* 4.

Berger, Bridget and Berger, Peter (1983) *The War Over the Family: Capturing the Middle Ground.* London: Hutchinson.

Bhachu, Parminder (1988) 'Apni, marzi, kardhi. Home and work: Sikh women in Britain', in S. Westwood and P. Bhachu (eds), *Enterprising Women: Ethnicity, Economy and Gender Relations.* London: Routledge. pp. 76–102.

Bhavnani, Kum-Kum and Coulson, Margaret (1986) 'Transforming socialist feminism: the challenge of racism', *Feminist Review,* 23: 81–92.

Brannen, Julia and Moss, Peter (1991) *Managing Mothers.* London: Unwin Hyman.

Brannen, Julia and Wilson, Gail (eds) (1987) *Give and Take in Families: Studies in Resource Distribution.* London: Allen & Unwin.

Britten, Nicky and Heath, Anthony (1983) 'Women, men and social class', in E. Gamarnikow, D. Morgan, J. Purvis and D. Taylorson (eds), *Gender, Class and Work.* London: Heinemann. pp. 46–60.

Brodribb, Somer (1992) *Nothing Mat(t)ers: A Feminist Critique of Postmodernism.* Melbourne: Spinifex.

Brownmiller, Susan (1976) *Against Our Will: Men, Women and Rape.* Harmondsworth: Penguin.

Bourdieu, Pierre (1990) 'La domination masculine', *Actes de la Recherche en sciences sociales,* 84.

Butler, Judith (1990) *Gender Trouble: Feminism and the Subversion of Identity.* New York: Routledge.

Carby, Hazel (1982) 'White women listen! Black feminism and the boundaries of sisterhood', in Centre for Contemporary Cultural Studies (eds), *The Empire Strikes Back: Race and Racism in 70s Britain.* London: Hutchinson. pp. 212–35.

Charles, Nickie (1990) 'Food and family ideology', in C. C. Harris (ed.), *Family, Economy and Community.* Cardiff: University of Wales Press. pp. 53–76.

Charles, Nickie and Kerr, Marion (1988) *Women, Food and Families.* Manchester: Manchester University Press.

Coonz, Stephanie (1988) *The Social Origins of Private Life: A History of American Families 1600–1900.* London: Verso.

Coulson, Margaret, Magas, Branka and Wainwright, Hilary (1975) '"The housewife and her labour under capitalism" – a critique', *New Left Review,* 89: 59–71.

Crompton, Rosemary and Mann, Michael (eds) (1986) *Gender and Stratification*. Oxford: Polity.

Dalla Costa, Mariarosa and James, Selma (1972) *The Power of Women and the Subversion of the Community*. Bristol: Falling Wall Press.

Davies, Bronwyn (1989) *Frogs and Snails and Feminist Tales*. Sydney: Allen & Unwin.

Delphy, Christine (1969) 'Le patrimonie et la double circulation des biens dans l'espace économique et le temps familial', *Revue Française de Sociologie*, 10: 664–86.

Delphy, Christine (1970) 'L'ennemi principal', *Partisans*, 54–5.

Delphy, Christine (1974) 'Mariage et divorce: l'impasse à double face', *Les Temps Modernes*, May.

Delphy, Christine (1975) 'Pour un féminisme matérialiste', *L'Arc*, April.

Delphy, Christine (1976a) 'Proto-féminisme et anti-féminisme', *Les Temps Modernes*, 346: 1469–500.

Delphy, Christine (1976b) 'Continuities and discontinuities in marriage and divorce', in D. Leonard Barker and S. Allen (eds), *Sexual Divisions and Society: Process and Change*. London: Tavistock. pp. 76–89.

Delphy, Christine (1976c) 'La transmission du statut à Chardonneret', *Revue d'Ethnologie Française*, 4 (1–2).

Delphy, Christine (1977a) *The Main Enemy*. London: Women's Research and Resources Centre.

Delphy, Christine (1977b) 'Nos amis et nous, des fondements réels de quelques discours pseudo-féministes', *Questions Féministes*, November.

Delphy, Christine (1978) 'Travail ménager ou travail domestique?', in A. Michel (ed.), *Les femmes dans la société marchande*. Paris: PUF.

Delphy, Christine (1979) 'Sharing the same table: consumption and the family', translated by Diana Leonard, in C.C. Harris (ed.), *The Sociology of the Family: New Directions for Britain*. Keele: Sociological Review Monographs. pp.214–31.

Delphy, Christine (1980a) 'Libération des femmes an 10', *Questions Féministes*, 7.

Delphy, Christine (1980b) 'A materialist feminism is possible', *Feminist Review*, 4: 79–104.

Delphy, Christine (1980c) 'Feminist glimmerings in Eastern Europe', *Feminist Issues*, 1 (1).

Delphy, Christine (1981a) 'For a materialist feminism', *Feminist Issues*, 1 (2): 69–76.

Delphy, Christine (1981b) 'Le patriarchat, le féminisme et leurs intellectuelles', *Nouvelles Questions Féministes*, 2.

Delphy, Christine (1981c) 'Women in stratification studies', translated by Helen Roberts, in H. Roberts (ed.), *Doing Feminist Research*, London: Routledge & Kegan Paul. pp. 114–28.

Delphy, Christine (1981d) 'Women's liberation in France: the tenth year', *Feminist Issues*, 1 (2): 103–12.

Delphy, Christine (1984) *Close to Home: A Materialist Analysis of Women's Oppression*, translated and edited by Diana Leonard. London: Hutchinson.

Delphy, Christine (1987a) 'Proto-feminism and anti-feminism', translated by Diana Leonard, in T. Moi (ed.), *French Feminist Thought: A Reader*. Oxford: Blackwell. pp. 80–109.

Delphy, Christine (1987b) 'Women's liberation: the tenth year', translated by Claire Duchen, in C. Duchen (ed.), *French Connections*. London: Hutchinson. pp. 33–44.

Delphy, Christine (1988) 'Patriarchy, domestic mode of production, gender and class', in C. Nelson and L. Grossberg (eds), *Marxism and the Interpretation of Culture*. London: Macmillan. pp. 259–67.

Delphy, Christine (1991a) 'Liberation des femmes ou droits corporatistes des mères?', *Nouvelles Questions Féministes*, 16–17–18: 93–117.

Delphy, Christine (1991b) 'Les origines du mouvement de libération des femmes en France', *Nouvelles Questions Féministes*, 16–17–18: 137–48.

Delphy, Christine (1991c) 'Penser le genre: Quels problems?' In M.-C. Hurtig, M. Kail and H. Rouch (eds), *Sex et genre: De la hierarchie entre les sexes*. Paris: Editions du Centre National de la Reserche Scientifique.

Delphy, Christine (1991d) 'Is there marriage after divorce?', in D. Leonard and S. Allen (eds), *Sexual Divisions Revisited*. London: Macmillan. pp. 45–58.

Delphy, Christine (1992) 'Mothers' Union?', translated by Diana Leonard, *Trouble and Strife*, 24: 12–19.

Delphy, Christine (1993a) 'Rethinking sex and gender', translated by Diana Leonard, *Women's Studies International Forum*, 16 (1): 1–9.

Delphy, Christine (1993b) 'L'etat d'exception: la derogation au droit commun comme fondement de la sphere privée', unpublished paper.

Delphy, Christine (1994) 'Changing women in a changing Europe: is difference the future for feminism?' translated by Diana Leonard, *Women's Studies International Forum*, 27 (2): 187–201.

Delphy, Christine (1995) 'The invention of French feminism: an essential move', *Yale French Studies*, 87, 1995 Special Issue: 'Another Look, Another Woman: the Reconstitution of French Feminism'.

Delphy, Christine and Leonard, Diana (1986) 'Class analysis, gender analysis and the family', in R. Crompton and M. Mann (eds), *Gender and Stratification*. Oxford: Polity. pp. 57–73.

Delphy, Christine and Leonard, Diana (1992) *Familiar Exploitation: A New Analysis of Marriage in Contemporary Western Societies*. Oxford: Polity.

Dezalay, Yves (1976) 'French judicial ideology in working-class divorce', in D.L. Barker and S. Allen (eds), *Sexual Divisions and Society: Process and Change*. London: Tavistock. pp. 90–107.

Duchen, Claire (1984) 'What's the French for political lesbian?', *Trouble and Strife*, 2: 24–34.

Duchen, Claire (1986) *Feminism in France: From May '68 to Mitterand*. London: Routledge.

Duchen, Claire (ed.) (1987) *French Connections: Voices from the Women's Movement in France*. London: Hutchinson.

Durkheim, Emile (1982) *The Rules of the Sociological Method*. London: Macmillan.

Dworkin, Andrea (1978) 'Biological superiority: the world's most dangerous and deadly idea', *Heresies*, 6. Reprinted as 'Dangerous and deadly' in *Trouble and Strife*, 14: 42–5, 1988.

Dworkin, Andrea (1981) *Pornography: Men Possessing Women*. London: The Women's Press.
Edholm, Felicity, Harris, Olivia and Young, Kate (1977) 'Conceptualizing women', *Critique of Anthropology*, 3: 101–30.
Fausto-Sterling, Anne (1989) 'Life in the XY corral', *Women's Studies International Forum*, 12 (3): 319–31.
Fausto-Sterling, Anne (1992) *Myths of Gender*, second edition. New York: Basic Books.
Féministes Révolutionnaires (1985) 'Patriarchal justice and the threat of rape', in d. rhodes and S. McNeill (eds), *Women Against Violence Against Women*. London: Onlywomen Press. pp. 35–9.
Ferguson, Ann (1989) *Blood at the Root: Motherhood, Sexuality and Male Dominance*. London: Pandora.
Finch, Janet (1983) *Married to the Job: Wives' Incorporation into Men's Work*. London: Allen & Unwin.
Finch, Janet (1989) *Family Obligations and Social Change*. Oxford: Polity.
Firestone, Shulamith (1972) *The Dialectic of Sex*. London: Paladin.
Flax, Jane (1990) 'Postmodernism and gender in feminist theory', in L. Nicholson (ed.), *Feminism/Postmodernism*. New York: Routledge.
Fouque, Antionette (1987) 'Interview with Antionette Fouque' (from *Le Matin*, 16 July 1980), in C. Duchen (ed.), *French Connections: Voices from the Women's Movement in France*. London: Hutchinson. pp. 50–4.
Fraser, Nancy and Bartky, Sandra Lee (eds) (1992) *Revaluing French Feminism*. Bloomington and Indianapolis: Indiana University Press.
Fuss, Diana (1989) *Essentially Speaking: Feminism, Nature and Difference*. New York and London: Routledge.
Gardiner, Jean, Himmelweit, Susan and Mackintosh, Maureen (1975) 'Women's domestic labour', *Bulletin of the Conference of Socialist Economists*, 4: 1–11.
Gilligan, Carol (1982) *In a Different Voice*. Cambridge, Mass: Harvard University Press.
Goldthorpe, John (1983) 'Women and class analysis', *Sociology*, 17 (4): 465–88.
Goldthorpe, John (1984) 'Women and class analysis: a reply to the replies', *Sociology*, 18 (4): 545–53.
Graham, Hilary (1987) 'Being poor: perceptions and coping strategies of lone mothers', in J. Brannen and G. Wilson (eds), *Give and Take in Families: Studies in Resource Distribution*. London: Allen & Unwin. pp. 56–74.
Guillaumin, Colette (1981a) 'The practice of power and belief in nature. Part 1: The appropriation of women', translated by Linda Murgatroyd, *Feminist Issues*, 1 (2): 3–28.
Guillaumin, Colette (1981b) 'The practice of power and belief in nature. Part 2: The naturalist discourse', translated by Linda Murgatroyd, *Feminist Issues*, 1 (3): 87–109.
Guillaumin, Colette (1987) 'The question of difference', translated by Claire Duchen, in C. Duchen (ed.), *French Connections: Voices from the Women's Movement in France*. London: Hutchinson. pp. 64–77.
Guillaumin, Colette (1995) *Racism, Sexism, Power and Ideology*. London: Routledge.
Haraway, Donna (1991) '"Gender" for a Marxist dictionary: the sexual politics of a

word' in D. Haraway, *Simians, Cyborgs and Women*. London: Free Association Books. pp. 127–48.

Harding, Sandra (ed.) (1987) *Feminism and Methodology*. Milton Keynes: Open University Press.

Harris, Olivia (1981) 'Households as natural units', in K. Young, C. Walkowitiz and R. McCullagh (eds), *Of Marriage and the Market*. London: CSE Books. pp. 49–68.

Harrison, John (1973) 'The political economy of housework', *Bulletin of the Conference of Socialist Economists*, Winter: 35–52.

Hartmann, Heidi (1981) 'The unhappy marriage of marxism and feminism: towards a more progressive union', in L. Sargent (ed.), *Women and Revolution: the Unhappy Marriage of Marxism and Feminism*. London: Pluto Press. pp. 1–41.

Harvey, Lee (1990) *Critical Social Research*. London: Unwin Hyman.

Hennessy, Rosemary (1993) *Materialist Feminism and the Politics of Discourse*. New York and London: Routledge.

hooks, bell (1982) *Aint I a Woman?* London: Pluto Press.

Hurtig, Marie-Claude and Pichevin, Marie-France (1985) 'La variable sex en psychologie: Donne ou construct?', *Cahiers de Psychologie Cognitive*, 5 (2): 187–228.

Hurtig, Marie-Claude and Pichevin, Marie-France (1986) *La différance des sexes*. Paris: Tierce.

Irigaray, Luce (1985) *This Sex Which is Not One*. Ithaca: Cornell University Press.

Irigaray, Luce (1993) *Je, tu, nous: Toward a Culture of Difference*. London: Routledge.

Jackson, Stevi (1992a) 'Towards a historical sociology of housework', *Women's Studies International Forum*, 15 (2): 153–72.

Jackson, Stevi (1992b) 'The amazing deconstructing woman', *Trouble and Strife*, 25: 25–31.

Jacobus, Mary, Fox Keller, Evelyn and Shuttleworth, Sally (1990) *Body/Politics: Women and the Discourses of Science*. New York: Routledge.

Jardine, Alice (1985) *Gynesis*. Ithaca: Cornell University Press.

Jardine, Alice and Smith, Paul (eds) (1987) *Men in Feminism*. New York: Methuen.

Joshi, Heather (1987) 'The cost of caring', in C. Glendinning and J. Millar (eds), *Women and Poverty in Britain*. Brighton: Wheatsheaf. pp. 112–33.

Kaluzynska, Eva (1980) 'Wiping the floor with theory: a survey of writings on housework', *Feminist Review*, 6: 27–54.

Kaplan, Gisela (1992) *Contemporary Western European Feminism*. London: UCL Press; Sydney: Allen & Unwin.

Komarovsky, Mirra (1950) 'Functional analysis of sex roles', *American Sociological Review*, 15 (4): 508–16.

Kuhn, Annette and Wolpe, Ann Marie (eds) (1978) *Feminism and Materialism: Women and Modes of Production*. London: Routledge & Kegan Paul.

Landry, Donna and MacLean, Gerald (1993) *Materialist Feminisms*. Oxford: Blackwell.

Laqueur, Thomas (1990) *Making Sex: Body and Gender from the Greeks to Freud*. Cambridge, Mass: Harvard University Press.

Leclerc, Annie (1974) *Parole de femme*. Paris: Editions Grasset.

Leonard, Diana (1980) *Sex and Generation: A Study of Courtship and Weddings*. London: Tavistock.

Leonard, Diana (1990a) 'Sex and generation reconsidered', in C.C. Harris (ed.), *Family, Economy and Community*. Cardiff: University of Wales Press. pp. 35–52.

Leonard, Diana (1990b) 'Persons in their own right: children and sociology in the U.K.', in L. Chisholm, P. Büchner, H.H. Krüger and P. Brown (eds), *Childhood, Youth and Social Change: A Comparative Perspective*. London: The Falmer Press. pp. 58–70.

MacKinnon, Catherine A. (1989) *Towards a Feminist Theory of the State*. Cambridge, Mass: Harvard University Press.

McLellan, David (ed.) (1977) *Karl Marx: Selected Writings*. Oxford: Oxford University Press.

Malos, Ellen (ed.) (1980) *The Politics of Housework*. London: Allison & Busby.

Marks, Elaine and Courtivron, Isabelle de (eds) (1981) *New French Feminisms: An Anthology*. Brighton: Harvester.

Marx, Karl (1976) *Capital Volume 1*. Harmondsworth: Penguin.

Mathieu, Nicole-Claude (1977) *Ignored by Some, Denied by Others: the Social Sex Category in Sociology*. London: Women's Research and Resources Centre.

Mathieu, Nicole-Claude (1980) 'Femininity/masculinity', *Feminist Issues*, 1 (1).

Mathieu, Nicole-Claude (1991) *L'anatomie politique: categorizations et ideologies du sexe*. Paris: Côté-femmes.

Maynard, Mary (1990) 'The re-shaping of sociology? Trends in the study of gender', *Sociology*, 24 (2): 269–90.

Maynard, Mary (1995) 'Beyond the "big three": the development of feminist theory in the 1990s', *Women's History Review*, 4(3): 259–81.

Maynard, Mary and Purvis, June (eds) (1994) *Researching Women's Lives from a Feminist Perspective*. London: Taylor and Francis.

Mead, Margaret (1935) *Sex and Temperament in Three Primitive Societies*. New York: William Morow.

Michel, Andrée (1959) *Famille, industrialisation, logement*. Paris: Côté-femmes.

Michel, Andrée (1960) 'La femme dans la famille française', *Cahiers Internationaux de Sociologie*, 111.

Mitchell, Juliet (1975) *Psychoanalysis and Feminism*. Harmondsworth: Penguin.

Mitchell, Juliet (1982) 'Introduction I' in J. Mitchell and J. Rose (eds), *Feminine Sexuality: Jacques Lacan and the École Freudienne*. London: Macmillan. pp. 1–26.

Moi, Toril (1985) *Sexual/Textual Politics*. London: Methuen.

Moi, Toril (ed.) (1987) *French Feminist Thought: A Reader*. Oxford: Blackwell.

Molyneux, Maxine (1979) 'Beyond the domestic labour debate', *New Left Review*, 116: 3–27.

Moores, Shaun (1993) *Interpreting Audiences: The Ethnography of Media Consumption*. London: Sage.

Morley, David (1986) *Family Television: Cultural Power and Domestic Leisure*. London: Comedia.

Murcott, Anne (1983) '"It's a pleasure to cook for him": food, mealtimes and gender in some South Wales households', in E. Gamarnikow, D. Morgan, J. Purvis

and D. Taylorson (eds), *The Public and the Private*. London: Heinemann. pp. 78–90.
Myrdal, Alva and Klein, Viola (1956) *Women's Two Roles: Home and Work*. London: Routledge & Kegan Paul.
Oakley, Ann (1972) *Sex, Gender and Society*. London: Maurice Temple Smith.
O'Brien, Mary (1981) *The Politics of Reproduction*. London: Routledge & Kegan Paul.
Onlywomen Press (eds) (1981) *Love Your Enemy: The Debate between Heterosexual Feminism and Political Lesbianism*. London: Onlywomen Press.
Oudshoorn, Nelly (1994) *Beyond the Natural Body: An Archeology of Sex Hormones*. London: Routledge.
Pahl, Jan (1990) *Money and Marriage*. London: Macmillan.
Parmar, Prathibha (1982) 'Gender, race and class: Asian women in resistance', in Centre for Contemporary Cultural Studies (eds), *The Empire Strikes Back: Race and Racism in 70s Britain*. London: Hutchinson. pp. 236–75.
Petty, Celia, Roberts, Deborah and Smith, Sharon (1987) *Women's Liberation and Socialism*. London and Chicago: Bookmarks.
Phoenix, Anne (1991) *Young Mothers?* Oxford: Polity.
Picq, Françoise (1987) 'The MLF: run for your life', translated by Claire Duchen, in C. Duchen (ed.), *French Connections: Voices from the Women's Movement in France*. London: Hutchinson. pp. 23–32.
Plaza, Monique (1978) '"Phallomorphic power" and the psychology of "woman": a patriarchal chain', translated by Miriam David and Jill Hodges, *Ideology and Consciousness*, 4. Reprinted in M. Brake (ed.), *Human Sexual Relations*. Harmondsworth: Penguin, 1982. pp. 323–59.
Poulantzas, Nicos (1973) 'On social classes', *New Left Review*, 78: 27–50.
Questions Féministes Collective (1977) 'Variations sur des thèmes communs', *Questions Féministes*, 1.
Questions Féministes Collective (1981) 'Variations on common themes', translated by Yvonne Rochette-Ozzello, in E. Marks and I. de Courtivron (eds), *New French Feminisms: An Anthology*. Brighton: Harvester. pp. 212–30.
rhodes, dusty and McNeill, Sandra (eds) (1985) *Women Against Violence Against Women*. London: Onlywomen Press.
Riley, Denise (1988) *'Am I that Name?' Feminism and the Category of 'Women' in History*. London: Macmillan.
Roberts, Helen (1993) 'The women and class debate', in David Morgan and Liz Stanley (eds), *Debates in Sociology*. Manchester: Manchester University Press. pp. 52–70.
Rubin, Gayle (1975) 'The traffic in women: notes on the "political economy" of sex', in R. Reiter (ed.), *Toward an Anthropology of Women*. New York: Monthly Review Press. pp. 157–210.
Ruddick, Sara (1980) 'Maternal thinking', *Feminist Studies*, 6 (2): 342–67.
Rushton, Peter (1979) 'Marxism, domestic labour and the capitalist economy: a note on recent discussions', in C.C. Harris (ed.), *The Sociology of the Family: New Directions for Britain*. Keele: Sociological Review Monographs. pp. 32–48.

Sauter-Bailliet, Teresia (1981) 'The feminist movement in France', *Women's Studies International Quarterly*, 4(4): 409–20.

Sellers, Susan (1991) *Language and Sexual Difference: Feminist Writing in France*. London: Macmillan.

Smith, Dorothy (1988) *The Everyday World as Problematic*. Milton Keynes: Open University Press.

Smith, Paul (1978) 'Domestic labour and Marx's theory of value', in A. Kuhn and A.M. Wolpe (eds), *Feminism and Materialism: Women and Modes of Production*. London: Routledge & Kegan Paul. pp. 200–19.

Smyth, Ailbhe (1983) 'Contemporary French feminism: an annotated shortlist of recent works', *Hecate*, 9: 203–36.

Stanley, Liz and Wise, Sue (1983) *Breaking Out*. London: Routledge & Kegan Paul.

Stanley, Liz and Wise, Sue (1993) *Breaking Out Again*. London: Routledge.

Stanworth, Michelle (1984) 'Women and class analysis: a reply to Goldthorpe', *Sociology*, 18 (1): 159–70.

Stoller, Robert (1968) *Sex and Gender: On the Development of Masculinity and Femininity*. New York: Science House.

Tabet, Paola (1982) 'Hands, tools, weapons', *Feminist Issues*, 2 (2): 3–62.

Thorogood, Nicki (1987) 'Race, class and gender: the politics of housework', in J. Brannen and G. Wilson (eds), *Give and Take in Families: Studies in Resource Distribution*. London: Allen & Unwin.

Tristan, Anne and Pisan, Annie de (1977) *Histoires du MLF*. Paris: Calmann-Lévy.

Tristan, Anne and Pisan, Annie de (1987) 'Tales from the women's movement', translated by Roisin Mallaghan, in T. Moi (ed.), *French Feminist Thought: A Reader*. Oxford: Blackwell. pp. 33–69.

Van Every, Jo (1995) *Heterosexual Women Changing the Family: Refusing to be a 'Wife'*. London: Taylor and Francis.

Walby, Sylvia (1986a) *Patriarchy at Work*. Oxford: Polity.

Walby, Sylvia (1986b) 'Gender, class and stratification, towards a new approach', in R. Crompton and M. Mann (eds), *Gender and Stratification*, Oxford: Polity. pp. 23–40.

Walby, Sylvia (1989) 'Theorising patriarchy', *Sociology*, 23 (2): 213–34.

Walby, Sylvia (1990) *Theorizing Patriarchy*. Oxford: Blackwell.

Walby, Sylvia (1992) 'Post-post-modernism? Theorizing social complexity', in M. Barrett and A. Phillips (eds), *Destabalizing Theory: Contemporary Feminist Debates*. Oxford: Polity.

Walby, Sylvia (1994) 'Is citizenship gendered?', *Sociology*, 28(2): 379–96.

Waters, Malcolm (1994) *Modern Sociological Theory*. London: Sage.

Weedon, Chris (1987) *Feminist Practice and Poststructuralist Theory*. Oxford: Blackwell.

Wittig, Monique (1980) 'The straight mind', *Feminist Issues*, 1 (1): 103–11.

Wittig, Monique (1981) 'One is not born a woman', *Feminist Issues*, 1 (2): 47–54.

Wittig, Monique (1982) 'The category of sex', *Feminist Issues*, 2 (2): 63–8.

Wittig, Monique (1985) 'The mark of gender', *Feminist Issues*, 5 (2): 3–12.

Wittig, Monique (1992) *The Straight Mind and Other Essays*. Hemel Hempstead: Harvester Wheatsheaf.
Witz, Anne (1992) *Patriarchy and the Professions*. London: Routledge.
Wright, Erik Olin (1973) *Class, Crisis and the State*. London: New Left Books.
Yeandle, Susan (1984) *Women's Working Lives: Patterns and Strategies*. London: Tavistock.

Index